Traditional Truth, Poetry, Sacrament
For My Mother, on Her 70th Birthday
Josef Pieper

ST. AUGUSTINE'S PRESS
South Bend, Indiana

Manufactured in the United States of America.

1 2 3 4 5 6   25 24 23 22 21 20 19

Library of Congress Control Number: 2019948036

∞ The paper used in this publication meets the minimum requirements of the American National Standard for Information Sciences -
Permanence of Paper for Printed Materials, ANSI Z39.48-1984.

St. Augustine's Press
www.staugustine.net

Josef Pieper Books Published by St. Augustine's Press

The Concept of Sin

The Christian Idea of Man

Don't Worry about Socrates

Death and Immortality

Enthusiasm and Divine Madness

Exercises in the Elements

Happiness and Contemplation

In Tune with the World

A Journey to Point Omega

Not Yet the Twilight

The Platonic Myths

Rules of the Game in Social Relationships

Scholasticism

The Silence of Goethe

The Silence of St. Thomas

The Sum Total of Human Happiness

Tradition

Tradition as Challenge

What Catholics Believe

What Does "Academic" Mean?

Tradition Truth, Poetry, Sacrament

Contents

About Listening and Philosophical Interpretation

It is not normally the case that a person, throughout the course of his life, carries out, step by step, a plan he has devised himself. But it may well happen that, as he looks back at his own work over a period of time, if all is going well he may see something that resembles planning and outcome. Of course, at the same time he will also become aware that he has not been the planner, but rather that he has followed the patterns of a plan that was not his. Yet, far from the plan being alien to him, it might have to be said that he himself is the plan.

There are three such patterns which stand out from the many kinds of endeavours which have preoccupied me over the last twenty years. They can be called "traditional truth," "poetry," and "sacrament." The first-named refers to what has been shaped and tempered in the course of tradition. It is the shape in which the mind, in search of the foundation of things, retains what it has found. "Poetry" stands not only for what is embodied in language, but for every poiema, for every "answer"—of all the fine arts—that has been given a shape. And "sacrament" comprises the whole sphere of cultic activity and sacred action. All three areas are in communication with one another by the fact that all of them expressly speak of the root and totality of the world and of existence.

This "speech," of course, which is shouted down by the noise of ordinary everyday "speech," is only audible under one presupposition. We have to attend to it in a particular way—otherwise, the message concerning the depths of our existence, and hence the meaning of "traditional truth," poetry, and sacrament, will remain unrecognizable and obscured.

At this point something needs to be said more in detail about the kind of attention required of us.

I am assuming that one presupposition is met: namely, that in all three—traditional truth, poetry, and sacrament—a "message" is contained which it is not only rewarding for a person to receive, but is also fitting and necessary; that he needs it for a meaningful and truly human life. — This applies to the sacramental, rightly understood, beyond all debate and most appropriately. As far as poetry is concerned, there is one restricting condition highlighted by Plato: it must be the work of "divine" poets. And, naturally, not every philosophical opinion can claim to be wisdom and traditional truth, even though, because brilliantly formulated or for some other reason, it may have survived in human memory. — So, again: we are presupposing that all the manifestations of things referred to by those three names will have "greatness" in the most demanding sense of the word. It will include things like "ultimate validity," "maturity," "worthy to be venerated," perhaps even "perfection."

It does not seem too difficult to characterize the attitude in which one appropriately attends to a "message" of this kind. It can hardly be anything other than an attitude of silent receptiveness, an attitude, therefore, of receiving, of hearing, of listening. This seems almost obvious. But what does it mean to be a listener?

The answer to this question, I think, is by no means obvious.

A person can follow with great attention what another person says—and yet does not listen to him. There is a difference between answering the questions of an investigating judge, holding a conversation at night with a friend, answering the questions of a qualified psychologist who is aiming to "test" me in an "exploration." No doubt, in all three cases one attends carefully to what is said. But who listens to me the way I—as the speaker—expect and as each of us naturally expects, even in dealing with an opponent?

A Platonic dialog can be read as a document of the Greek language or as a document of Athenian life at the time of Socrates. It can certainly be read with an eye to the history of philosophical thinking: how much information about sophistry can be taken from a work such as the "Gorgias" dialog. Naturally, "Gorgias," like every human opus, is a biographical document and can therefore be read under this aspect as a document of the "period of transition" from the early dialogs to those of the period of mature mastery. With regard to the concluding myth in "Gorgias" about judgment in the next life, the question can be discussed whether, for example, this particular version of the three judges stems from Orphism or from the Egyptian Books of the Dead. One can ask why Plato placed this myth at the end of the conversation between Socrates and the power politician Callicles; and the answer could be: "because his artistic sense needed a metaphysical background as a complement to the heroic isolation of the Socratic soul." One can intentionally see in the doctrine of the pre-existence of the soul an argument for saying that Plato, before writing his "Meno," must have become acquainted with the Pythagorean tradition in southern Italy. And so on.

These are all examples taken from scholarly works on Plato. And they are, without exception, examples of not listening. I am not saying that it is inadmissible or unimportant to ask and to discuss such questions, just as I do not think it is inadmissible for a person to be tested. But these are not cases of "listening." It is not a case of sitting at Plato's feet but of looking over his shoulder. But our presupposition is that Plato is a man of such rank that it is proper and worthwhile to sit at his feet and listen.

It is easy to see that the way of handling the work of great writers, as described above, is quite the usual one.

Let us suppose that the author of the brief "Meditation" included below under the title "The Greater World" was not myself but an historically well-known author who lived five hundred years ago. Let us suppose, furthermore, that an industrious editor was not only the first to bring to light this tiny forgotten opusculum but, on the basis of his profound knowledge of the work, of the not yet published correspondence and likewise not published diaries, together with lecture schedules and seminar reports etc. etc., had also proved: that the work had been written down at very short notice [which would explain certain irregularities in the development of the argument]; that the author, at the time of writing, gave a university lecture on the subject of justice; that "peace" was also a theme which rose out of it; and that, on the other hand, the theme can be explained, in this special formulation, by the fact that in a lecture cycle beginning around the same time the article was taken from the Summa theologica of Thomas and used as an example of the structure of a scholastic quaestio: "Whether concord and peace are the same thing." It becomes clear that the quotations are for no very good reason declared to be utterances of a great teacher of Western Christendom, are statements entirely taken from Thomas Aquinas; they are to be found reproduced in their entirety in the notes which accompany the edition and with exact references. Light is also shed on seemingly insignificant things with the utmost diligence: for example, diary entries giving witness to an intensive reading of Dante give plausibility to a gratuitous quotation from the Divina Commedia; to say nothing of the fact that certain peculiarities in vocabulary and syntax are convincingly interpreted as the individual style of precisely this author. — Undoubtedly, such an "interpretation" which in its theme, style and aim has nothing unusual about it could justifiably be referred to as a worthy academic achievement. And even the author of that innocent opusculum would have to agree. Of course, if I were in his position I would not reject the criticism: that in this interpretation there is not the slightest evidence as to whether the content and the real point of the "meditation" had been heard, taken seriously, and considered—in other words, whether the interpreter had "listened" to his author.

But how are we to conceive of such "listening"? What is distinct about it, how can we recognize it? — Let us speak directly again about Plato: for example, his teaching formulated in the "Meno" and "Phaedo" dialogs that the soul must have lived before this bodily existence and must have contemplated the essences of things. How could I "listen" to this teaching? Is it possible for a person of our time, for a Christian, to take the content of this Platonic view seriously? I think it is possible. Listening is not the same as agreeing, nor does it presuppose agreement.

What is presupposed, however, is that we accept the question itself. I can only listen to the teaching about a pre-existent soul if I take seriously the question to which this teaching is the answer—the question about how human knowledge came into being at its beginning, the beginning which happened prior to all of our concrete experience. This is by no means a question to which "in the meantime" we have been able to provide a clear and final answer. A person who does not ask this question himself is not really able to "listen" to the problem that Plato is faced with: namely, that the purely empirical does not provide a sufficient solution; that, as Socrates says, it is necessary to turn to those who are "wise in divine things"; that, finally, on the basis of theological "information" about immortality that includes both the past and the present it can be assumed that, before all possibility of experience in this life—with priority in time and in essence—the soul has access to the sphere which houses the archetypes of things. No one who seriously considers these things would think himself in a position to look over the shoulder of Plato, this ancestor of all Western philosophizing.

Real listening is therefore linked with the presupposition that I do not derive the question originally from Plato (or Aristotle, or Augustine, or Thomas, etc.) but that this questioning has already been kindled, and the flame has been fed—continuously—through contact with the reality which confronts me directly: today's reality.

The truth of this is seen every day. Anyone who is not "interested" in what is said is not able to listen—at least not in the way that the person speaking naturally expects. Anyone who wanted to "listen" to his partner in conversation the way that imaginary interpreter "listened" to his author—attending mainly to his style of speaking, his voice inflection, the expression on his face, the origin of the images he uses and of his thoughts—would be insulting the speaker and assaulting his dignity. Strange as it may seem at first sight, it is nevertheless true: no one who is speaking simply to another person can wish that this person wants formally and exclusively to learn what he, the speaker, is thinking and saying. Instead, what he wants is that the listener considers his words, which means that he measures the content against what he holds to be true. Even contradiction is more welcome to the healthy mind than that curiosity about the speaker as such. The dignity of the person expressing himself in words is preserved by the listener's not focusing on him but on the content of what he says. Is this not what is meant by Socrates' words, spoken in the face of death, to his friends who are gathered in his prison cell? His argument for immortality is not fully clear to them, but they are careful not say out loud the counter arguments they are whispering amongst themselves ("… we did not want to unsettle you in your present wretched state"). His word of admonition was: "Don't worry about Socrates; worry about the truth."

Thomas speaks in similar terms. He juxtaposes two questions: one is about "what others have thought" and the other is about "finding out what is the truth of things." This utterance has, as we know, been cited in many books and articles. But it has seldom been noticed that the incisiveness of the statement is only revealed when the particular context in which it occurs is taken into consideration. It is found in a commentary (on Aristotle)—in a book, therefore, which has no other aim than to find out what an "other" has thought. This surely means that Thomas is of the opinion that it is possible in such a way to try and find out "what others have thought" but that at the same time the real focus remains directed on "finding out what is the truth of things."

When Thomas calls this attention to the truth of things "philosophical" and when one, with some justification sees the other kind of question ["what others have thought"] as concerned with history—the further question arises about the way that the philosophical mode of questioning is to be seen in relation to the historical one. But that is a new theme which I cannot develop here.

These remarks are not concerned with "On the Use and Abuse of History for Life" (Nutzen und Nachteil der Historie für das Leben) but rather with some presuppositions which must be met, if, in dealing with the great figures, a fruitful listening and a philosophical interpretation are to be achieved. Undoubtedly, one of these presuppositions is a certain level of historical knowledge. There is historical knowledge which makes listening easier, intensifies it, or makes it possible in the first place. But it is not a question of proportion, such that when one element increases the other must also become stronger. Clearly the ancients knew what they were saying when they spoke in this context of a contrast.

Thus it is a very important fact that an Aristotle commentary, unsurpassed to this day, had as its author a man who not only did not know Greek but also had no notion of the genesis of Aristotle's metaphysics which he thought was planned as a unified book, whereas history teaches us that it is a somewhat chance collection of very diverse pieces. This man is Thomas Aquinas. Now why is this an important fact? What "follows" from it? We want to answer with the utmost caution. First of all we need to take into consideration that Thomas is a brilliant interpreter and that, in addition, he is linked with his author Aristotle in an unusually profound and fundamental relationship. It is, of course, unquestionable that Thomas might have written an even more superb commentary, if, instead of using a more or less adequate Latin translation he could have based his work on the critical Oxford edition of the text by W. D. Ross. But what is especially important is clearly this: that it is not impossible really to listen to a voice even when it is not clearly audible; and that this listening, primarily aimed at the "truth of things," despite that lack of clarity, can result in an exposition—not only of what is heard but also of the world as a whole—which is penetrating to an extent that is hardly ever achieved despite the most advanced perfection of historical text criticism.

But there is a still more serious fact to consider. A more accurate historical knowledge does not simply enable or even promote a more intensive, more fruitful listening; it can also have the effect of hindering it.

It is reported of countries under the sway of bolshevism that permitted editions of works by Plato or Dante are published with a preface which provides the reader with an "historical" understanding and openly aims at preventing the reader from taking the works seriously. Of course, such explanations are not to be considered real "history." However, what is said in these prefaces is less crucial than the shifting of the reader's gaze from the content of the work to the author and to things that condition his utterance. The important point is to prevent listening. — But is this prevention not a quite general phenomenon? Does not exactly the same apply, to a large extent, to scholarly historical writing about Homer, Plato, Sacred

Scripture, and the traditional treatment of the liturgy?—namely, the mere hearing, the direct experience, hinders or prevents the wordless openness in receiving? It is true that questions come into play here which are not even explicitly posed, let alone answered. But however they are to be formulated and whatever the answer must be, the essence of our modest reflections remains untouched: only someone who reads the great writers like Plato, Virgil, Thomas without asking "what others thought"; only someone who approaches a poetic or even a sacred text in such a way that he is not really bothered with the author, the textual history, the source of the material but only about the answer, the light, the instruction—the truth—only he is really listening. Only a person who, confronted with the timeless shape of traditional truth, poetry, and sacrament, directs his inner gaze to the hidden root of the world and of life—only he is able to perceive and share the "message."

I

Not only the saints but also the philosophers say:
the ultimate happiness and bliss of God, angel,
and man is to see God.

Thomas Aquinas

Knowledge and Freedom
(1953)

The formulation "Science and Freedom," in today's context, is aimed at an opponent who theoretically denies the freedom of science as well as consciously endangers, limits, and destroys it.

But when this antagonism involves an intellectual debate and not a mere "demonstration" (the dramatic change in meaning of this word "demonstration" has a hidden relevance to the theme!), it is then necessary for the opposite position to be known not only in the form of its concrete manifestation, but in its roots. Only then can clarity be expected about the kind and strength of argument that would be a sufficient counter to the intrinsic thrust of the opponent's view.

This is not meant so generally and in such a "purely academic" way as may at first seem. — Since the beginning of critical literature about bolshevism, it has been said again and again that bolshevism is by no means a strange phenomenon which suddenly emerged, but rather that it basically expresses "the secret, hidden world view of middle-class society—for example, the absolutizing of economic activity; that the East formally draws conclusions from what the West in fact thinks; that in our very justified battle against the Soviet slave state we are impeded by one thing": namely, that the same tendency is alive in our own society. Those are quotations chosen at random from an historical-critical work about bolshevism, from a report about imprisonment, and from a polemical pamphlet about freedom. Naturally we are dealing with exaggerated formulations, yet they show us that in intellectual debate about bolshevism we must be aware that the situation is complex.

It could happen, for example, that for the sake of refuting the opponent it suddenly becomes necessary to revise one's own presuppositions. I believe a person particularly likely to have this experience is one who undertakes to explore the exploitation of scientific knowledge by the totalitarian worker state. More precisely: anyone who challenges this exploitation by which the freedom of knowledge is infringed on—anyone who opposes this not by way of political struggle and active or passive opposition but by way of intellectual debate (and only this concerns us here)— such a one finds himself confronted with arguments which he can only refute by correcting, at the same time, some notions which have been accepted and taken for granted in Western civilization for centuries. These are notions which contradict ideas, the validity of which has been unchallenged in the West; they contradict that which not alone the great teachers of Christendom—Augustine no less than Thomas Aquinas—but also Plato and Aristotle have thought. These old and those new notions all concern our theme very precisely: namely, the meaning of knowledge as such and the link between knowledge and freedom.

What I would like to propose, positively, is the following: in order to counter the decline in scientific freedom as it is found in the totalitarian worker state an effective argument can only be found, in the sphere of intellectual debate, if at the same time some fundamental insights are brought into play which were formulated in the pre-modern Western tradition.

We must now speak of these insights, if only in a somewhat summary form. One of them—the most important one—is expressed in Aristotle's *Metaphysics*. On the first pages of this book, which may be described as one of the "canonical" works produced by the Western mind, freedom of knowledge is mentioned. But, to be more precise: it is said of a particular kind of knowledge, of a particular endeavour to know, that it is, amongst all branches of knowledge, free in the highest degree; and that this is "obviously" the case. This refers to knowledge concerned with the whole of reality, with the structure of the world as a whole. What is meant is consideration of the question about the essence and fundamental being of things. It is the application of our knowing faculties—from deep within our spirit—to the totality of all that is, to the meaning and foundation of all reality in toto: i.e., the application of the mind to its complete and undiminished object. What is meant is "knowledge as such," which is not limited to anything in particular but which, however, includes all individual acts of knowledge applied to the concrete or to a particular aspect of reality—and therefore also scientific knowledge. In brief, this mode of knowledge is what Aristotle here calls the "most peculiarly philosophical." It becomes apparent that here we are not dealing with some separate form of metaphysics (Aristotle does not know and does not use this expression at all). Instead, it is a question of the impetus of our knowing power as a whole, which is at work precisely in all concrete experiences and in the conclusions we draw, gathering and including them all as it seeks out the object appropriate to it: the whole.

This kind of knowledge is what Aristotle says is the only free kind. The question is: what does "free" mean here? We are touching here the critical, neuralgic point of the problem. "Free" according to Aristotle (and here he is formulating what is probably an entirely ancient idea, which was used, for example, by his teacher, Plato, and which later exerted a commanding influence on the whole of Western thought)—"free" means as much as "non-practical." Praxis means the achieving of aims; that which serves to achieve an end is "the practical." But only the kind of knowledge which deals with the ultimate foundation of the world is supposed not to "serve" a purpose (that is the general opinion); it is (supposedly) not even possible or thinkable to put it to any use: "it alone is there for its own sake." Now exactly this not being there for anything else, but for itself and for its own sake—this is what human language sees as "freedom."

But in this unbelievably concise paragraph of a little more than twenty lines in Aristotle's *Metaphysics* some further characteristics of that free and non-practical knowledge are added and should not be omitted. Aristotle adds the following: the knowledge that focuses on the totality of the world, purely for the sake of knowing and to that extent free—this knowledge cannot possibly be achieved by man; he never fully grasps it; it is therefore not something that man possesses without limitation, since as a human being he is himself subject to many kinds of necessities. He must serve. One would have to say that only God can achieve this knowledge completely, just as it is also the divine root of all things to which this knowledge aspires. For this very reason no other kind of knowledge has the rank and dignity of philosophical knowledge, although they are all more necessary:

necessariores omnes, dignior nulla (as the Latin version of the ancient Greek puts it). So much for Aristotle.

That is the sketch of a world view in which the concept of "scientific freedom" has its origin. But with "origin" we are not merely referring to the historical source, although this, too, has to be considered, for it is indeed the case that in the second chapter of Aristotle's *Metaphysics* the two concepts of "freedom" and "knowledge" are considered in relationship to one another in the history of Western thought. A thousand and a half years later, Thomas Aquinas, in his commentary on this same chapter, formulated the definition of the *artes liberales* (from this term the medieval name of the philosophical faculty—Arts Faculty—derives its name). And if, exactly one hundred years ago, John Henry Newman, in his book which has since become a classic, *The Idea of a University*, speaks of "liberal knowledge or a gentleman's knowledge," he is explicitly placing himself in the same tradition.

But more important than the historical derivation seems to me to be the fact that the concept of, or rather the claim for "scientific freedom" has to lose its legitimation and its inner credibility when it becomes separated from its origin: namely, from the foundation of that world view. This is, I believe, what has happened at the beginning of the modern age.

The fundamental world view, which is, of course, more a view of the essence of man and the meaning of his existence, can be expressed briefly as follows:

First: however much man is a practical being who needs to use the things of the world to meet his requirements for living, he does not acquire his real riches through technical subordination of the forces of nature but through the purely theoretical knowledge of reality. The existence of man is all the richer the more deeply he has access to reality and the more it is opened up to him. Through his knowledge he achieves the purest realization of his being, so that even his ultimate perfection and fulfilment consist in knowledge; Eternal Life is called a *visio*. — This is not a notion derived specifically from Christian theology. It is found also in Aristotle. Anaxagoras expresses it in his own way when, in answer to the question "why were you born?" he says: "To look at the sun, the moon, and the sky"—by which he would not have meant the physical heavenly bodies but the construction of the world as a whole.

Second: because man, in his theoretical knowledge, is doing—more than in any other way—that which he fundamentally and really wants to do (and this is what the concept of "freedom" really consists in: doing what one wants to do!), not only is his "knowledge" to be termed "free," and all the more so the more it is theoretical; but also *man himself* is freer, the more his knowing is theoretical, directed to truth and nothing else. This accords with experience: anywhere that a person, independently of looking after life's immediate goals, approaches reality purely as a knower; wherever, without being worried about usefulness, damage, danger, death, he is able to see and to say: "That is how it is and not otherwise" ("The Emperor has no clothes on")—in these circumstances human freedom is realized in a special sense. Truth makes you free, as the venerable saying has it.

In the West, this has been re-formulated again and again. Martin Heidegger is also speaking from within the same tradition when he situates the essence of truth in freedom.

Three: There are levels of knowledge—and therefore

also of the freedom realized in knowing. The highest level would be attained if our knowing faculties grasped their object completely; in this case the most extreme level of freedom would be realized; man would be doing, in the most perfect way, what he really wants. But I am using a hypothetical subjunctive. This goal cannot be achieved by man in his bodily existence in history, although it is what keeps the whole thrust of this same existence in motion. That is Aristotle's meaning where he says: the question about the foundation of reality as a whole "is one which always and ever, and today, is posed—a continually open question." The medieval commentator, Thomas Aquinas, made this profound remark about the statement: precisely because the answer cannot be at our disposal as our own, this wisdom is sought after for its own sake (included here is the statement that we cannot seek the answers as ultimate answers once and for all—in the way they are to be found in the exact sciences. Not in the full sense of "for their own sake," not as something meaningful in itself in the highest possible way.)

At this point something very incisive is being said, I believe, about science [in the narrower sense]: despite the exactness of its answers it is not the highest form of knowledge. And also with regard to freedom it occupies a middle position, an almost ambiguous one. This is seen in two ways—*first point*: man's self-limitation to scientific knowledge in the strict sense can mean that he loses his openness for the unlimited object of knowledge. In other words: there is a particular form of intellectual un-freedom, the root of which is the exclusive ideal of science. *Second point*: it is not contrary to the nature of science to be used for purposes which are extrinsic to it. No injustice is done to science if it accepts tasks emanating from the sphere of praxis—whether this be political, economic, technical, or military. This does not destroy science; whereas philosophy, because it is concerned with the whole of reality, the object of knowledge which is sought after simply for its own sake, would be *eo ipso* destroyed by such employments. One can think one is taking philosophy into service, but behold!—what is taken into service is no longer philosophy! Of course, there is also in science, at its inner core, an element which cannot be pressed into service: that is the philosophical element of *theoria*, which is geared to truth and nothing else. That means that science has, by its very nature, a claim to freedom to the extent that it is not practical, but theoretical.

This is the quintessence of all that we know so far: freedom of knowledge is closely bound up with—indeed, identical with—its theoretical character. Anyone who infringes on scientific freedom or destroys it can do this only by infringing on or destroying its theoretical character. On the other hand: anyone who surrenders the theoretical character of knowledge or declares it unessential by comparison with practicality is passing up the possibility of defending any claim to scientific freedom. We are put in this strange position by some theses proposed at the beginning of the modern era which have become a constituent part of modern consciousness. We can admit that these theses came to light not without legitimate reasons, and yet we can still consider that they are false or at least in need of correction. I am thinking here of the sentence in Descartes's *Discours sur la méthode* that a new, "practical" philosophy needs to replace the old theoretical one in order to put us in a position to become masters and owners of nature (par laquelle ... nous pourrions ... nous rendre comme maîtres et possesseurs de la nature)—a thought which recurs almost word for word in the thesis of American pragmatism, that all human knowledge has the character of being a tool in the context of the "intellectual industry"; that "giving security to life and enjoyment of life is the aim of all intellectual activity"; that, above all, philosophy is ultimately not aimed at acquiring knowledge of the world but at finding ways to control it. I will quote a third thesis: "A scientist who is preoccupied with abstract problems should never forget that the aim of all science consists in satisfying the needs of society." No one will want to say that there is a difference, in principle, between the thesis represented by Descartes and Dewey on the one hand and, on the other hand, the last thesis I have quoted—taken, rather cunningly!, from the *Great Soviet Encyclopedia*.

In all of these theses the theoretical character of knowledge is openly denied. (Anyone, furthermore, who approaches reality exclusively with the attitude of "how do I become master and owner?" is simply not capable of focusing purely theoretically—i.e., being concerned with truth and nothing else—with the totality of the world and with the essence of things.) — But freedom has also become impossible; more accurately, it has become impossible to defend it with any credible argument.

If science in the totalitarian worker state finds itself in the situation where it continually has to answer the inquisitorial question: what is your contribution to the Five-Year-Plan?—this is nothing but a strictly drawn conclusion from Descartes' thesis about the philosophy of the maître et possesseur de la nature.

We see here an extreme possibility which no longer seems totally foreign to our experience. If we no longer have certainty that knowledge of truth is what makes the spirit free, it can perhaps come about that the concept of freedom itself is questionable and beyond the grasp of our minds: we don't know what it means. — Thus one reads with concern, in the last diaries of André Gide, the entry: "Thousands are prepared to sacrifice their lives to bring about a better standard in living conditions: more justice, a more equal sharing of earthly goods; I scarcely dare to add: more freedom—*because I don't know exactly what is meant by it.*" — But we can pass over the question of how this strange note is to be interpreted.

My only aim has been to make clear that the concept "scientific freedom" is rooted in rich soil, perhaps deeper than expected, and that a radical attack like the one we are dealing with at present requires its defenders to consider this origin.

There is an important sentence which, in a moving way, names this origin: the ultimate form of freedom of the knower. The sentence is significant, above all, because of the man who spoke it and because of the particular situation in which he wrote it down. The man is, in the most distinguished way, a Western figure: a Roman who did his studies in Athens and then, at the court of a Germanic prince, sought to communicate the wisdom inherited from antiquity to the new age that was looming: Boethius. But the situation is that of a prisoner. From his prison cell where he awaits his execution, Boethius assures himself of his ultimate, indestructible freedom, saying: "The human soul is necessarily at its freest when it remains in contemplation of the divine spirit."

On the Desire for Certainty (1953)

Certainty contributes to the gravitas of knowledge. That is an old saying, but one which had special significance for the ancients. At first this seems clear, even obvious: I only "know" something properly when I know it with certainty and reliably. And it is not difficult to establish this fact. We are not dealing here with something which only concerns the scholar (although it does also concern him in a particular way); no, it concerns man's relationship to reality as a whole. Knowing, knowing about, seeing—that is the basic form of all relationships with reality. All human intellectual relationships to the world are rooted in knowing, in this fundamental mode of grasping being and taking hold of the world. In asking about the perfection of our knowledge and our knowing, I am at the same time asking about a greater or lesser perfection of one's relationship to the world, of contact with reality, of one's grasp of being. My relationship to my world is "in order," has its ultimate rightness and perfection, when it is based on certainty, i.e., when I am absolutely sure of the fundamental things which concern me and when I have them in my grasp unmistakably and with complete assurance—which means that I am absolutely certain about them. Certainty contributes to the gravitas of knowledge!

I said that this saying had special significance for the ancients. The situation here is somewhat confusing and cannot easily be clarified. The ancients did not exactly reject the idea, of course not; but they did add an extremely important modification.

There are several possible answers to the question about what perfection of knowledge consists in. One answer is: knowledge is perfect when absolute certainty is attained. This is the only answer of which we have spoken so far. But would not also the following answer be conceivable: knowledge is perfect when the highest possible fullness of being can be seen, the highest possible object, reality of the most perfect kind? These two answers are radically different from one another. The second of the two determines the level of knowledge in relation to the object, in relation to the world of objects, in relation to the level of reality that has come within the grasp of the knower. The first of the two answers says: it is precisely the degree of this comprehensibility and accessibility that determines the level of knowledge. We are concerned in this respect not with the level of the object but with the certainty and reliability of access, with the exactness of possession—in a word: with certainty.

This answer characterizes the thinking and philosophy of the modern period, as does the fundamental attitude which has emerged: concern of the knower with the reliability of the knowledge, with certainty and with the level of certainty which can be achieved. Saying this is almost a platitude. Philosophizing in the modern era begins with Descartes' fundamental question: what is ultimately certain? What can resist doubt? Kant belongs to this lineage when he says that the theme of metaphysics is: what can I know? Can I know anything with certainty? This led

Nietzsche to refer to all of more modern philosophy as a "school of suspicion."

And what do the ancients say—the great teachers of Christendom, the founders and patriarchs of the Greek tradition of wisdom? In a *summa* of the High Middle Ages, we find another sentence juxtaposed—or even opposed— to the sentence "Certainty contributes to the gravitas of knowledge." It is an uncommonly significant sentence, which far exceeds the ambit of our present inquiry: "The slightest knowledge that one can have about the most sublime things is more desirable than the most certain knowledge of lesser things." As we can see, the language is extremely plain. At first sight it is so lacking in "interest" that, in hearing or reading it, one is inclined to think there is nothing "special" about it. But it is all too easy to move around on the untroubled surface of this very clear pronouncement without realizing what profound depths lie beneath it. I said the sentence is to be found in a medieval *summa*; in antiquity there are quite similar, almost identical formulations. I quote, for example, from Aristotle: "We have only meagre knowledge of the sublime and divine things ... But: even if we are able to have only the slightest contact with these higher regions, this kind of knowledge, because of its greater dignity, is more desirable than all things in our own world—just as there is more bliss in having the slightest glimpse of a beloved person than in contemplating, very closely, much else and even important things."

What is being said here? First of all, it is immediately clear how fundamentally different the angle is from which this is spoken: it is not primarily a question about certainty but about the reality. It is not a question about our relationship to the world but about the world itself. Here there is no suspicion, no mistrust; on the contrary, there is very definite trust in being—certainly not a "naïve" trust (as one might for a moment think). To see things more clearly here, we must consider another element of the ancients' insight. It is the following: human knowing faculties are understood as finite, as non-absolute, as limited. Is this not also the case, and even especially the case, in the attitude of mistrust and suspicion which characterizes the beginnings of modern philosophy with its methodic doubt? It might seem so; but I believe this is a deception. Behind the mistrust of the doubter there is something other than acknowledgement of the limitations of the human creature's understanding. Is there not instead the intention and the expectation and the claim, through critical caution, through a methodically exacting discipline, to achieve—precisely—absolute certainty? Against this, on the other hand, a fundamental attitude is expressed in that sentence of the ancients, which says: there are no absolute certainties except for the absolute mind. "No one on earth"—as John Henry Newman formulated it—"no one on earth can give strictly adequate evidence for drawing an absolute conclusion." Precisely the highest reality is, for the natural capacity of our human knowing powers, the most difficult to grasp with any certainty; precisely the realities which are in themselves the most translucent and certain are for us the most obscure and the most uncertain: our knowledge is all the more uncertain the more its object is perfect; it is all the less certain the more it touches and concerns us. — The ideal of precision in methodic doubt, on the other hand, is based on the claim that man has to be able to be sure about the objective validity of being by having absolute certainty—which can be achieved, of course, only with difficulty and through effort—whereas the ancients say: the subjective certainty of the human spirit cannot, on principle, be seen as a measure of our objective certainty about reality. Anyone who insists exclusively on criticism and exactness is thereby saying: it must be possible for man, by avoiding and rejecting all non-exact methods, to attain to absolute certainties—whereas the opinion of the ancients is: perfect the exactness of your methods as much as you can and will, but you will never achieve absolute certainty.

Thus it is not as if the problem of certainty did not exist for the ancients. They have not a word to say against the statement: "Certainty contributes to the gravitas of knowledge." But they see the problem regarding certainty—*concretely*. Which means: they ask who is certain of what? If this "who" is man, and therefore a non-absolute, created being—then there is no absolute certainty, because by its essence the created spirit can never comprehend anything in the strict sense (comprehend means, in the formulation given by Thomas in his Commentary on John's Gospel, to know something to the extent that it is knowable in itself, i.e., to exhaust all knowability and to convert it into the known, to know something totally and "once and for all"). Since this is only possible for an absolute creative spirit (only one who creates can comprehend), for a human spirit there can be no last, ultimate absolute evidence.

Therefore one could say: mistrust as found in the ancients delves much deeper into the human capacity to know, is much more radical than the suspicion entertained by the methodic doubter, for whom nothing can be exact enough—one *could* say this if this more radical mistrust was not founded on a still more profound trust. In this form of mistrust there is an imperturbable affirmation;

one could even go so far as to speak of the cheerfulness connected with not being able to comprehend, a cheerfulness which is closely related to humor and which is based on the fact that man knows that he is a not-absolute being—a creature. If one has this self-understanding that precisely as a knower he is creature (not-absolute, finite, dependent, one who by his very nature receives)—such a one cannot take the problem of certainty so seriously, as something so existentially important that he always goes back to the question: can I be certain of that? Such an attitude would make it impossible to lead a really human life–because it would fundamentally contradict the essence of man as creature. The claim to absolute certainty contains not only something which is fundamentally humorless but even formally un-human, for it implies the unwillingness to accept the status of receiver. It contains the error (or should one say: the heresy, the self-deception, the deliberate error?), that the human spirit can, of itself, penetrate into the ultimate depths of things in reality—at depths where things could be so comprehensible in themselves that they cease to be something we simply accept. But it is not possible for us to live like this—for in this way we do not arrive at the object. (As one of Goethe's late letters formulates it: critical philosophy "never arrives at the object. We have to admit this, just as normal human intelligence does, in order to enjoy life through our unchanging relationship (to the object).") Surely everyone knows that the impoverished object, the thinness of what is said through it, is a characteristic accompaniment of extreme exactitude. If "certainty" is the exclusive criterion of genuine knowledge, that is the scarcely avoidable consequence—a consequence, by the way, which is perhaps readily accepted, even risked, once a high level of precision is achieved on the level of form of a statement, in other words of certainty. But against this, from the other angle, the question must be asked whether, for the sake of such minimal content, such a measure of exactness is worthwhile.

This, too, is a legitimate point of view: what is worthwhile? It is not only a question of what can be known but of what is worth knowing. There are things that can be known very exactly but are scarcely worth knowing at all. The "Science of the Not-Worth-Knowing" is not a completely unreal notion. For this we have no need to clutch at Strindberg's "Knobology." The ancients speak of "sublime" and "lower" things (whereby we must immediately add that in this latter expression no rejection, nothing judgmental is implied. Characteristic of "hierarchical" thinking which acknowledges genuine rankings is that all the lower levels are affirmed and acknowledged). Anyone who is only concerned with certainty forgoes the possibility of distinguishing between things which are more worth knowing and less worth knowing: for him, everything is worth knowing if it can be known exactly. From this angle it is not possible to criticize the "Science of the Not-Worth-Knowing" and to show resistance to it. Such criticism is only feasible where the level of being of things is important for evaluating human knowledge.

This is precisely the meaning of the old proposition: "The slightest knowledge we can attain about the most sublime things is more desirable than the most certain knowledge about lower things." This does not merely mean that knowledge of sublime things is of higher worth than knowledge of lesser things (no one would want to dispute this); nor does it mean: knowledge of lesser things is of lesser value than the knowledge of great things even where the lesser things are known more completely, more clearly, more certainly, and more exactly. No, the meaning here is even more extreme, something really challenging: namely, the lowest level of certainty is more desirable, more "to be longed for" than the highest level of certainty—if the highest level relates to the lesser things and the lowest level to the most sublime.

Is There Such a Thing as a Non-Christian Philosophy? (1952)

It seems to make sense to ask whether there is a Christian philosophy. After all, philosophizing means using one's reason in a very radical way; philosophizing means asking what is the meaning of all that we call "life" or "reality" or simply this "totality." Now if someone already has an answer to this question about meaning, if one "believes," if one is a Christian: how can he still really use his reason in the very radical way mentioned? How could he still be able to philosophize? Is there such a thing as Christian philosophy? — To ask this question would seem meaningful.

However, our question is whether there is a non-Christian philosophy. — And now, to say the worst from the outset I am inclined to answer: no, there is no non-Christian philosophy! — But is this not simply absurd? For, apart from India and China ... Stop, here I have to add an explanation: I am slightly inclined (to be more precise) to answer: no, in the Western world, in Europe there is no non-Christian philosophy—insofar as (another modification!) we understand by philosophy what the great originators and fathers of Western philosophy, Pythagoras, Plato, and Aristotle understood it to be.

And what did they understand it to be? Naturally it is not possible to present the concept of philosophy of these great men with all its ramifications. But two important elements of this concept need to be discussed. First point: the literal meaning of the word philosophy, philo=sophia, should not be treated as merely anecdotal. Plato, at least, saw as fundamental the legend according to which Pythagoras is supposed to have said that a person cannot be called wise, but at most he can be called one who lovingly seeks wisdom (not a Sophos, but a philosophos). The essential philosophical question is about the search for a wisdom which—in principle—we can never "have" as a possession as long as we are in our present condition of bodily existence. And then: what kind of wisdom is it which we are in principle not able to achieve and for which we do not give up our loving search (cannot give up)—what kind of wisdom might that be? The Pythagorean and Platonic answer is quite clear. It is wisdom as God possesses it: God alone can be called wise in the full sense; He alone has "the answer," the interpretation of reality from one angle (namely, from Himself); no one but God knows what the philosophical question deals with: the whence and the whither, the origin and the goal, the design principle and the structure, the meaning and the organization of reality as a whole. — This first element of the Greek concept "philosophy" has, in principle, a simple relationship to theology—an openness, in principle, to theology.

And what is the second element? It is the following: when I pose a philosophical question and consider what is knowledge fundamentally, what is man, what is real?, but also: what is, ultimately, this piece of matter which, in the form of a sheet of paper, I have in my hand?—

whenever I ask questions like this I am at the same time asking about the structure of the world as a whole; with such a question I am confronting reality as a whole, and in contemplating that philosophical question I must speak of "God and the world." The scholar in any particular discipline does not need to do this. Someone who seeks to find the cause of a particular contagious disease does not need to speak of God and the world (he should not); but anyone who asks: what is sickness as such—ultimately—will not succeed in dealing adequately with, and do justice to his subject if he does not want to speak of God and the world. He must literally begin with Adam and Eve. He cannot, for example, ignore the problem of "sickness and guilt," "organic sickness and inner moral disorder" (naturally, he does not need to say that sickness is always connected with moral disorder—far from it—but he must speak of the possibility of the connection): but what is guilt and moral disorder? How can anything of consequence be said in this regard if we are not to speak of it in the context of God and the world, of "Adam and Eve"? This means that seriously to ask a really philosophical question we are not able formally to ignore any kind of truth, insight, or knowledge of any kind of reality—whether it is information we have from the exact sciences or from faith or theology (naturally, as long as such theological information is valid as information about reality!). If in discussion of a philosophical question one were to exclude in principle—for example, for the sake of some kind of methodical purity—particular aspects of truth and were not to speak, say, of God and the world, one would, by the same token, cease to be pursuing a philosophical inquiry. One would no longer really be inquiring about ultimate being, about the deepest root of things, i.e., one would have destroyed the really philosophical character of the inquiry.

We should note that this is Plato's view. It is not a "Christian" interpretation. It is an element of the concept of philosophy as developed in antiquity. It is Socrates who says we have to stick to the information given us by those who are wise in divine matters: namely, to the information given us by priestesses and priests, and also poets (so many of whom are divine)—if we want to be clear about what learning and teaching fundamentally is. It is Plato who, in discussing the question of what love, Eros, really is, tells the story of the original fall of man, of the loss of original wholeness of the human being—a story which is undoubtedly "theology." And now if anyone had tapped Plato on the shoulder and pointed out to him: here you have transgressed your boundaries, this is no longer "pure" philosophy, but precisely theology, faith, revelation, myth—we could imagine that Plato would have looked surprised; and his answer would have been: the true philosophizer is not interested in philosophy but in the roots of things. And if you reject knowledge which comes from the myth about the root of things, about the ultimate essence of Eros, how am I to believe that you are seriously inquiring into the foundation of things?

But what follows from this for our inquiry? Firstly, this: if, with regard to philosophy, we are concerned with wisdom as God possesses it (and this is said not only by Pythagoras and Plato but also by the much more "scientific" Aristotle who calls the philosophical theory of being precisely theology because God alone fully and perfectly possesses the answer sought here); and if, furthermore, it is characteristic of philosophical inquiry that no information about the foundation of things—no matter where it comes from—can be excluded, least of all the information in which, as in mythical tradition and in theology, precisely that wisdom—as God possesses it—in some way seems to be within our grasp: then "Christian philosophy" is not only something we can take for granted but it is also precisely necessary, simply as the genuine, natural form of philosophy in this world of ours, as long as by philosophy we mean what Pythagoras, Plato, and Aristotle meant by it. And indeed how could such fundamental concepts as wisdom and searching for wisdom need to be corrected or made to fit in with progress through the ages?

It is very easy to respond to the question whether there is a Christian philosophy—a question which usually amounts to a challenge or criticism. From the angle of Plato's philosophy there is nothing that needs to be defended or justified. Much more difficult to answer—hardly answerable at all—is the other question: in our Western civilization which has been shaped by Greek culture and by Christianity, how is a non-Christian philosophy possible? The question seems unanswerable, or rather: must not the answer be that a non-Christian philosophy is not possible—that there isn't one? How can that be so? Why not? Because all the truth and wisdom which for Pythagoras, Plato, and Aristotle was contained in their mythical tradition has gone—subsumed into the teachings of the Christian tradition! There is no more information about the world of a super-rational kind. There are no longer any myths about the world which are really believed in and which the philosophizer can fall back on. There is no genuine tradition any more—except Christian tradition! *That is simply a fact of experience.* And does it not mean that only by reference back to Christian theology is it possible for philosophizing to retain that contrapuntal many-sidedness of what the world tells us which Platonic philosophizing possessed by virtue of being close to myth?

But what about modern philosophy? Does it mean that it is not at all real philosophy? Here we need a distinction. Today there is an approach to philosophy which does not at all claim to be philosophy in the old Platonic sense. But? But a kind of academic subject which is of interest to specialists but has no human concern and is not relevant to any thinking person. Logistics, for example, is such an academic discipline; but it is clearly not something associated with what has been traditionally understood as philosophy. — But what about existentialism? It obviously does not find its roots in Christian theology; but is it not philosophy? The relationship of existentialism—Sartre's existentialism, for example—to Christian theology is very complicated and not at all easy to define. However un-Christian Sartre sees himself to be, a Greek, a sophist, a nihilist like Gorgias would not be able to read him. I think a person from antiquity would not understand Sartre because for that you would need to be a Christian! "There is no human nature because there is no God who could have designed it"—how could a pre-Christian Greek be expected to understand this Sartrean proposition? That is how much his philosophy has to do with Christianity! Yes, but would it not be absurd to call Sartre a "Christian philosopher"? It would, of course, be absurd. And so there is—even in our Western world—philosophy which is not Christian and is yet genuine philosophy undoubtedly of interest both to the specialist and to the non-specialist?

This is precisely the question which I hesitate to answer in the affirmative: can philosophizing of this kind, deprived of its relationship to a true theology, still be called philo=Sophia; is it still really a loving search for wisdom? One can only search for something which one supposes really exists and which, somewhere and some-time, can also be found.

Mystery and Philosophy
(1950)

In what follows we will not be concerned with what philosophy or particular philosophers teach about the subject "mystery." Instead, we will be concerned with the concept of philosophy and philosophizing insofar as it has its own particular relationship to mystery.

1

In the good times of philosophical awareness, which, of course, seem to be coming to an end, it was sometimes forgotten that the concept of philosophy and philosophizing was from the beginning seen as a negative concept— at least more negative than positive. I have no need to repeat here in detail the well-known story about Pythagoras, the ancient legend according to which this great teacher from the 6th century BC coined the term "philosopher": God alone can be called wise, and man can at best be referred to as one who lovingly seeks wisdom. Plato also speaks of the contrast between wisdom and philosophy, between sophos and philosophos. In "Phaedrus" he has Socrates say: Solon and Homer should not be called wise men. "Phaedrus, that seems to me too great a thing, something that could only refer to a god; but to call them philosophoi would seem right and appropriate." And

Diotima, who in the "Symposion" expresses the most profound Platonic thoughts, expresses the same idea in a negative formulation: "None of the gods philosophize."

But what does all this mean if not that philosophy and philosophizing are, from the very beginning, understood as something that is *not* sophia, *not* wisdom, *not* knowledge, *not* understanding, *not* possession of truth?

This kind of thinking, however, is not peculiar to Pythagoras and Plato. No. Aristotle, the founder of critical and scientific philosophizing, goes further along the same path, at least as far as metaphysics is concerned—which is the most philosophical discipline. And Thomas Aquinas, in his masterly commentary on Aristotle's *Metaphysics*, repeats the view of the great Greek in very precise terms, where he says: metaphysical truth about being is not something for man to have as a possession [non competit homini ut possessio] but as a loan [sicut aliquid mutuatum]. Thomas then gives this idea further speculative justification with unfathomable profundity. Here all we can do is refer to it. He says, namely, that wisdom cannot be the property of man for the very reason that it is sought after for its own sake; what we can fully possess cannot satisfy us as something sought after for its own sake; the only wisdom that is sought after for its own sake is the kind that man is not able to have as a possession.

It is not as if, according to Aristotle and Thomas, man is cut off from any relationship to Sophia—this is precisely not the case. Philosophical questioning concerns precisely that kind of wisdom; philosophical questioning aims at comprehending, at ultimate knowledge. But—and this is said, of course, with great emphasis: not only do we not possess such knowledge, but we are even, on principle, incapable of possessing it, and therefore we will also not possess it in the future. By contrast, we will doubtless be able to acquire answers relating to individual disciplines (but these, on the other hand, cannot satisfy us in such a way that we would seek them "for their own sake"). It is an essential aspect of the philosophical question that it is inquiring about the ultimate essence, the ultimate meaning, the deepest roots of something that is real. The model of a genuine philosophical question is: what is, fundamentally, man as such, truth, knowledge, life, or whatever else? Now this implies that this kind of questioning, by its very nature, is looking for an answer which contains and expresses the essence of what is inquired about—completely and undiminished. Such an inquiry demands an answer in which, as Thomas says (in defining what "comprehending" means), the thing is known to the full extent that it is knowable in itself. In other words: the adequate answer to the philosophical question would have to be an answer which exhausts the subject, a statement in which the knowability of the object in question is exhausted to such an extent that nothing purely knowable remains but only the known. I said that this would be an "adequate" answer to a philosophical question; "adequate" means here that the answer corresponds formally to the question; but let us remember that the question is directed at the ultimate essence and the deepest roots of something that is real. The philosophical question is aimed, by its very nature, at the answer given where there is comprehension in the strict sense. But, according to Thomas, there is nothing at all that we can comprehend—unless it is our own work (to the extent it really is our own work: the marble itself is not the work of the sculptor!).

All of this means that a philosophical question, by its very nature, cannot be answered in the same sense as it is posed. — In this regard Plato, Aristotle, Augustine, and Thomas are in complete agreement with the great tradition of the human race as a whole. And it would be a rationalist aberration from the philosophia perennis if one wanted to overlook this negative element in the original concept of philosophy. Let us look again at the tradition of the philosophia perennis to see whether it justifies making such an unusual and perhaps even outrageous statement.

Aristotle says very solemnly and with a, so to speak, non-Aristotelian formulation that the question about being is open—"it always was, is today, and always will be." Thomas commented on this statement not only without any trace of criticism, but he himself says similar things. For instance, the efforts of all philosophers have not yet managed to discover the essence of one single gnat. And how often, in the *Summa theologica* and the *Quaestiones disputatae de veritate*, does the sentence recur: we do not know the essential distinctions between things—which means that we do not know the essence of things themselves. And that is the reason that we are unable to give them any essential name. Thomas even speaks of the imbecility of our intellect, from the stupidity of our mind which is not capable of "reading" from things in nature what is revealed in them about God.

Thus it seems as if Thomas—in a very extreme formulation—has expressed not only the basis for a *theologia negativa* ("This is the utmost level of human knowledge of God, to know that we do not know God—since we know that God's essence lies far beyond what we know of Him"), but he has also expressed the principle of a *philosophia negativa* (a formulation which perhaps can be more easily misunderstood and abused than that of the *theologia negativa*).

This essential distinguishing characteristic of a philosophical question—looking for an answer which cannot adequately be given—makes it different from questions posed in the exact sciences, which have, in principle, a different relationship to their object. It is normal for an individual science to formulate its question in such a way that it can be answered or at least that it is not, in principle, unanswerable. One day medical science will know, once and for all, what causes cancer. But the question about the nature of knowledge, about spirit, about life, the question about the ultimate meaning of this whole wonderful and terrible world—these questions will never be answered by philosophy once and for all, even though they are posed in a philosophical way. What is sought after in the genuinely philosophical question is explicitly knowledge about the supreme cause (in which knowledge, as Thomas says, wisdom as such consists); but philosophy, on its loving search, will *remain* on its journey as man and humanity are themselves on a journey, in statu *viatoris*. Thus the claim to have found the "formula of the world" is without hesitation to be called unphilosophical. It is of the essence of philosophy that it cannot be a "closed system"— "closed" in the sense that the essential reality of the world could be adequately mirrored in it.

2

But what becomes of this "negative" element of philosophy if philosophy becomes Christian philosophy? As we know, it is not unusual for people to think that Christian philosophy is superior to a non-Christian philosophy by virtue of the fact that Christian philosophy is in possession of clear, ultimate answers.

But this is not the case. Christian philosophy does have an advantage, or at any rate could have an advantage. Nevertheless, this superiority does not consist in its having final, ultimate, exhaustive answers to the philosophical questions. Then what is the advantage? — Garrigou-Lagrange says, in his beautiful book about sense for mystery, that it is indeed a distinctive characteristic of Christian philosophy not to have easy solutions, but—to a higher degree than in every other philosophy—to have a sense for mystery. But again, what does this difference mean; how could that be a basis for superiority—if even Christian philosophy itself does not find an ultimate solution to problems?

The superiority claimed here consists in a higher degree of truth. There is a higher degree of truth in a deeper awareness that the world and being are themselves mystery and therefore inexhaustible. The deeper one's positive knowledge of the structure of the world the more one becomes clear that reality is mystery. The reason for this inexhaustibility is that the world is creature, i.e., that it has its origin in God's incomprehensible, creative knowledge. It is the peculiarity of all being that it is the fruit of creative divine knowledge which is absolutely and infinitely superior to all human knowledge—this is the character of all being that emerges all the more compellingly the deeper the insight one has. Thus one can suppose that reality, through the experience that it, as creature, is inexhaustible, will be more profoundly known than in any lucid and seemingly closed system of theses.

But does not recourse to theological truth make an ultimate solution possible? Let us pose a counter question: is it not the meaning—and the salutary meaning—of theology to prevent human thought from arriving at conclusions which, perhaps in their abstract clarity could act as a powerful temptation and seduction but do not reflect the mysterious and complex structure of reality? Such a "hindrance," which in fact is a great benefit, does not make Christian philosophy less intellectually complicated; rather, one could say that complication is a distinguishing hallmark of Christian philosophy. If Thomas has recourse to theological arguments, that is not with a view to producing smoother arguments but to breaking out of the methodical prison of the "purely philosophical" and to open up to the genuine impetus of philosophical questioning—transcending the contradictions in our natural thinking—the sphere of revealed mystery.

Mystery—that does not refer to anything exclusively negative. It is not just darkness. Strictly speaking, mystery means something that is not darkness. It means light—but such fullness of light that human knowledge and human language cannot "drain" it. Mystery does not mean that our thinking endeavour comes up against a wall, but that, on the contrary, this endeavour penetrates into a sphere of creation which in its breadth and depth is wide open.

Thus the claim to pre-eminence of Christian philosophy lies in its call to find deeper insight into both at once: into the fullness of truth and into the inexhaustibility of truth. Insight into the shortcomings of human knowledge grows in proportion to the growth of this knowledge itself.

Science may quite rightly limit itself to the sphere of what can positively be known. But philosophy, the very nature of which is to inquire about the foundations of reality and thus to push forward into the dimension of its createdness, has formally to do with the incomprehensible, with creature as mystery.

Philosophy and the Common Good (1952)

For the perfection of human society it is necessary to have people who devote themselves to the vita contemplativa—as the ancients say.

Eight out of ten people reading this statement today will find it incomprehensible or simple false; and hardly anyone—perhaps one in ten—would find contemplation "necessary," and certainly not "socially" necessary, even if the contemplative life seemed to him something quite meaningful and respectable. — Besides: what would that opinion of the ancients have to do with the theme "Philosophy and the Common Good," since quite clearly contemplation is not philosophy?

The following thoughts, however, are based on the conviction that the ancient statement about the social necessity of the vita contemplativa is, firstly, unreservedly true and, secondly, exactly relevant to our theme.

But it is here already clear that there is no point in further argument until what is meant by the "common good" is explained and also what is meant by "philosophy."

I am opening Plato, the ancestor of all Western philosophy. Socrates says of the wise men of the past and also of himself that the philosophizer should keep his distance from affairs of state; the sophist, Protagoras, sees the "philosophy" he teaches as something that enables one to be active in word and deed in the city state (which means that Plato himself holds a different opinion); the sophist's pupil, Callicles, says: Anyone who preoccupies himself with philosophy when he is no longer a youth will miss out learning what is needed to gain power and honor in the state (which again means, though not in the same sense, that Plato himself has a different opinion); and again, Socrates: the true philosophizer often does not even know where the town hall is, and in the courthouses he cuts a quite laughable figure. Adding to this the consideration that the two most voluminous works of the same Plato—and the most truly philosophical ones, in the highest sense—are the "Politeia" and the "Nomoi," which deal with nothing but the ordering of political society, we sense the objective intricacy of our problem just as well as the need to clarify our fundamental concepts.

So, what does "common good" mean? And what is "philosophy"?

"Common good," bonum commune: that is the "good" concerned with the well-being of the human community and is the reason why the community exists; it is the embodiment of the values which a community— above all, the state community—would have to realize if one could say that it has realized its possibilities. This is, of course, a purely formal and abstract designation. It becomes really interesting when one tries to say what is the content of the bonum commune in the concrete world. Then it becomes apparent that this cannot be said exhaustively and once and for all, for this would presuppose that one could, with exhaustive finality, say what possibilities lie in a human community and what it fundamentally is. And it is not possible to say this, no more than it is possible to say definitively and once and for all what man is—

for which reason no one can exhaustively say, in terms of content (materialiter), what the "good" of man is that constitutes the reason for his existence and that he would have to realize in his life if it could be said of him that he has realized his possibilities (ultimately this is what Socrates means in the "Meno," for example, with his doggedly defended statement: he does not know what "the virtue of man" is and he has never met anyone who did know). All of this does not mean that it is impossible to say anything at all about the concrete content of the bonum commune, but rather that what is to be stressed is that such statements cannot have an exhaustive and ultimate character.

Perhaps at first sight this idea might seem purely "academic," but in reality it has contemporary political significance.

It is essential to every totalitarian regime that the one who has political power undertakes to determine the concrete content of the bonum commune. The danger with the five-year plans is not the attempt to bring production and need in line with one another. The real danger consists in making the "plan" the exclusive benchmark for all aspects of life—for mining as well as for the University syllabus, for the organizing of free time as well as for the artistic production of painters, poets, and musicians—so that everything that cannot be justified by this benchmark is declared to be "socially insignificant" and "undesirable," if it is not simply forbidden and suppressed.

But there is another characteristic of contemporary social planning: the plans are, naturally, almost exclusively based on usefulness. That means that the concept of the "common good" is explicitly narrowed down to mean "common usefulness"—so that the claim to define bonum commune exhaustively and definitively says, in addition, that only what is useful contributes to the well-being of human society.

The disturbing thing is that that which happens in the modern totalitarian worker state—explicitly and in a radical form—is happening in the whole world, although not explicitly and less radically. It is disturbing that in the whole world this imperceptibly increasing identification of "common good" with "common usefulness" is taking place. This can be seen in, amongst other things, the fact that philosophy and philosophizing are considered more and more as a mere intellectual luxury, as something which is barely compatible with "social conscience"—a kind of sabotage of one's "really important" tasks. This step is not in the slightest surprising. It is, in fact, simply unavoidable—if "common good" is the same as "common usefulness," for philosophy is defined precisely as not belonging to the sphere of usefulness. If, on the other hand, the ancients said philosophy was necessary ("necessary for the perfection of human society"), this was only possible because they understood that the concept "common good," while including "common usefulness," also included more—as the whole includes the part but is more.

This brings us back to our theme, the discussion of which, as we have seen, throws up fundamental questions.

But we still have to say more clearly what philosophy is. Is it really the same as contemplation (which up to this point seems to have been implicitly presupposed)? Yes, in some respects philosophy is contemplation. Cicero and Seneca used contemplatio as the Latin translation of the Greek theoria. And theoria is indeed the inner core of philosophy. But what is theoria? The ancients' answer was that theoria is an engagement with the world which aims at nothing but truth, an attitude of silent listening, distinct, above all, from the attitude of one actively realizing goals. Theoretical means precisely non-practical. But is there not also theoria in every genuine branch of knowledge, like physics or sociology? There is. But the realization of theoria is only "pure" in philosophizing. Every branch of knowledge is constituted by approaching reality with a definitely formulated question—which is why it is in this respect not silent. The philosophizer, on the other hand, who wants to know what all that is is fundamentally about, what "reality" "really" means—one who seeks this kind of knowledge does not start out with a definitely formulated question in the way a scientist does. Precisely this attitude of wordless listening enables him, on the one hand, to see all information from every branch of knowledge as a contribution to the answer he is really looking for; on the other hand, it disposes him not to be satisfied with any of these items of information but to remain open to the ultimate "wisdom," aspiring to which is central to the concept of philo=sophia.

But is there not also such a thing as practical philosophy? No. The really philosophical form of philosophy, the philosophical doctrine of being—the "first philosophy" (as Aristotle meant it)—can certainly not be practical. "All knowledge that is wisdom and is called philosophy is knowledge for its own sake: it is therefore theoretical and not practical." This is what Aquinas says in his commentary to Aristotle's Metaphysics. All intellectual life, even all praxis, originates in the pure process of becoming conscious of reality, and the philosophical aspect of philosophy is precisely that it is the place where this process is nurtured.

This means two things: something negative and something positive.

— The negative: it is not possible to philosophize for the sake of realizing some sorts of goals. That is impossible by the very nature of the thing. The positive: in the purely theoretical, philosophizing engagement with reality man can achieve freedom which cannot be had elsewhere and in any other way, and in which even the fact of external lack of freedom can possibly be irrelevant. — This is the reason why the ancients referred to the man devoted to theoria as "blissful" in a special sense. It is the inner freedom from looking after concrete needs, the satisfying of which is the function of praxis. (Naturally, in the long run man cannot exist in this way; but in the moments of theoria he succeeds again and again in transcending the sphere of the everyday.)

So here we have some essential elements of the concept of "philosophy."

At this point an objection is raised: when Descartes, in line with Bacon, demands a "practical philosophy" he is clearly formulating a different kind of philosophy which seems to overcome and cancel out the conflict (of philosophy) with the world of practical living as the ancients see it. Reply: if philosophizing means that man is preoccupied with the roots of things, the ultimate meaning of being, the real sense of "all of this," the Bacon/Descartes approach—the approach of the philosophy of the modern era—must indeed be understood as philosophy destroying itself. Anyone who thinks of reality as the raw material of human activity cannot even start to ask the question about the roots of things—the really philosophical question—no more than one can love a person other than for himself.

Another objection: is this separation and tearing apart of theoria and practice not meaningless? — Reply: if we insist on retaining the purity of theoria, i.e., of its indifference to praxis, we are thereby defending the fruitfulness of theoria and proclaiming the link between theoria and praxis.

As I already said: all praxis deserving of the name of "human activity" comes from the pure process of becoming aware of reality. This is the meaning of Goethe's words: "In our deeds and actions everything depends on the objects being purely grasped and treated according to their nature." Praxis is based on an engagement with reality which aims at becoming aware of reality, i.e., of truth and nothing else. In other words: theoria is only fruitful for praxis as long as it is not concerned with being fruitful.

Seen in this way, there is also a certain indirect relationship—one that is certainly difficult to formulate—between philosophical theoria and "ordinary practicality." Naturally we still have to consider that the theoretical element in individual branches of knowledge, despite being a philosophical element, is nevertheless not real "philosophy."

But this still does not explain the full sense of the statement quoted at the beginning, according to which, philosophy is necessary for the perfection of human society. — To show this necessity and to give it a clearer formulation we need first of all to say what real philosophizing results in, to what insights it leads. Then it may be possible to say what philosophy "does" for the common good—the latter being understood, naturally, as distinct from "common usefulness."

I am trying to imagine the ironic look of puzzlement

Socrates would have on his face if he were to have heard this question. But also Aristotle, who with his systematic mind is rightly called the founder of a more "scientific" philosophy, says that it is of the nature of a philosophical question that it is brought closer to a solution but that it can never be answered once and for all. This is not to say that philosophizing despairs of meaning, but, on the contrary, that it is characterized by hope. Of course, hope also includes the negative element that sophia—the ultimate answer—cannot be already in our possession as belonging to us. And, in fact, which of the philosophical questions— What is the real? What is man? What is knowledge?—has found an answer to match the finality associated with the discovery that the TB bacillus is the cause of pulmonary consumption? According to Thomas Aquinas, the efforts of philosophers have not yet succeeded in fathoming the nature of a single gnat.

And so, what is philosophizing "good" for?

Is not precisely this already something good for us to find, again and again, that being, the world, reality— which I cannot possibly give up pondering—is unfathomable? I am unable to get to the bottom of it. The more I know about things, the further the sphere of the not-yet-known stretches out in front of me as immeasurable. Do we perhaps not *need* precisely the fact that we are again and again prevented from forgetting that the world—including the self—is a mystery? Experiences of this kind certainly do not make us "capable"; they amount to us being "profoundly moved." But we are not properly human if we are not able to be profoundly moved by becoming aware of the deeper aspect of the world. And so this would be the role of philosophy: to help man to experience again and again, along with the mysterious character of the world, his own unfinished state, the not-yet of his own being and existence—and this despite all the skill and fascinating perfection of scientific knowledge and achievement which continually seduces the "lord and owner of nature" into taking too shallow a view of himself and the world.

Are there, then, no objective philosophical outcomes, no insights which could be expressed in propositions? And how would the answer "no" be reconcilable with the classical teaching of the philosophia perennis? There are, in fact, objective philosophical insights which can be formulated in propositions. But they do not amount to a "system," and certainly not to a "closed system" which could lay claim to be an adequate reflection of the essential reality of the world. In the great tradition of Western philosophy, the objective outcome of philosophizing which can be formulated in propositions has always been considered "scant," although Thomas Aquinas says in his commentary on Aristotle's *Metaphysics*: the little knowledge that can be achieved in the "First Philosophy" is of more weight than all else that can be known in the sciences.

Experience of the mysterious character of reality is not a mere negativum, no more than is the "I know that I don't know" of Socrates; when it is a really knowing encounter and not a merely vague feeling, this experience penetrates deeper and finds a "truer" truth about the world than any exact science can do. Only a discerning encounter with the mystery—which consists in the fact that something is—only this experience gives us the awareness that the light which makes things "positively" knowable, is simply unfathomable and inexhaustible and thus, at the same time, makes things incomprehensible.

Science has to do with the positively knowable aspect of things; philosophy is formally concerned with the underlying incomprehensibility. Therefore philosophical knowledge, although it cannot be formulated in terms of a positive outcome or an "answer," is nevertheless the deeper truth.

What does philosophy contribute to the common good? — The answer will depend on our conception of what is "good" for man, for the individual as well as for the community, and on what is of real value to him. The opinion of the ancients (Plato, Aristotle, Augustine, Thomas) seems to me highly significant: that man's true and genuine advantage is not that he can satisfy his daily needs, not that he can be the lord and proprietor of nature and its forces. The "noblest form of possession," the most genuine way to conquer the world, is through knowledge of reality.

The more the world becomes accessible and opened up, the richer our existence. This applies not only to the individual but also to the community: society, too, lives from truth manifested "publicly" in a higher or lower degree. That does not mean, of course, that politics, as the endeavour to achieve the common good, is not first and foremost concerned with satisfying basic needs, with the preservation of external peace and the country's internal order, and with harnessing the forces of nature. But the ancients say: all of this is a necessary presupposition, but only a presupposition for man taking possession of the things that are of real value to him. And so philosophy is not merely a part of the common good, but because in philosophical theoria, in contemplation, and in it alone (not in science) the unfathomable, divine foundation of things is accessible and the mastery of reality in the highest sense takes place, the enabling of contemplation is the objective of politics: "It is"—as Thomas says in the Commentary on Aristotle's Nicomachean Ethics—"the joy of vision, felicitas speculativa, to which all political life seems to be oriented."

Soliloquy on Hope
(Easter 1951)

"There is only one really serious philosophical problem: suicide. To consider life worth living or not worth living is to answer the fundamental question of philosophy. Everything else—whether the mind has nine or twelve categories—is secondary, mere trifles. First we need an answer." The author of these words is Albert Camus. Their radicalness is marvellous and it goes to the heart of the matter—the eternal question about the inner existence of man.

But: when, under what conditions is life worth living? Life means being on the way—when is it meaningful to continue the journey? When there is a reason to hope! Hope for what? That the journey, to say it with caution, does not lead to futility. But, speaking less cautiously, what does that mean positively?

What is new in Albert Camus's statement is that it demands such a radical answer, one that is fundamental, to do with life and death. This is new and is, of itself, a reason for hope. So, what does it mean: it makes sense to live, there is a reason to hope—and a reason so weighty that, even for someone already on the point of pushing life away it could serve as rich soil from which a newly planted existence could spring? With astonishment we heard recently in the last volume of poems by Wilhelm

Lehmann—a distinguished poet—exclaim to his friend who was "tired of life on earth" and who already "had his hand on the latch":

> The summer's day has brewed the air
> Ambrosia, basil and savory
> ...
> The plums are splitting, ripe for the mouth
> The sun-dial points only to the cheerful hour.

Impeccable verses, yes. But it is astonishing to hear them precisely from this poet, who (as Goethe says of himself) was well acquainted with despair. Or are we dealing here with despair? Can a person in our time seriously believe it is possible, by referring to the surrounding air and the light of the external world, to call back a person for whom the world has grown dark within him? "Is there reason to hope?" "But look, it is spring again, with crocus and hazel in bloom and the song of the hedge sparrow!" This answer is simply not enough. Above all, it does not reach the man. This is only heard by someone who previously has already heard another, deeper, more radical answer. But someone who has not accepted this prior answer is deaf to the glorious voice of spring. And so it seems that the poetic voice of Wilhelm Lehmann is less convincing than the cry of despair of Sartre's Orestes: "Let the flowers wither when I die!" The melodious sound of the world does not reach the ear of the person in despair. But what could reach him? What can be said to him—if calling and saying and pointing can achieve anything at all? What kind of argument would it have to be to induce him to change his mind? (We do not give up our belief that he is in error; that there is an argument; that there is a completely adequate counter-argument—we do not give up this belief; but it is, of course, "belief"!)

And so, again: how is there any reason for a person to say (no, not only to *say*): All will work out well in the end—for myself and for the world as a whole. It will be a *good* end, "good" as such. We should say it with the Diotima of Socrates, the way she describes fundamental beauty: "*not* just good in one respect and not=good in another respect; *not* just good for a time but then again not=good; *not* seeming good to one person and not=good to another." How can there be reason to suppose that the end will be such perfect fulfilment that all longing will be satisfied, so that, objectively and subjectively, there is nothing left to desire? Is there, in the end, well-being and bliss in the ultimate sense, i.e., once and for all? If not, it would not be possible to say that there is any reason for hope at all; anything less does not satisfy the inner claim of our existence—and the argument we are searching for against despair must have this kind of weight.

Naturally, arguments will be no help to the person in despair—not just words, no matter how true they are. He must not just see that there is reason to hope. He would need to be brought to the point of *hoping* (which is something different!). But how would that happen?

There is, of course, no point in offering private opinions on such a subject. We should investigate the wise teachings found in tradition.

But what does tradition say?

The first element is that there is salvation (as Kierkegaard says, there is nothing very clever in the words: there is eternal life!). This first statement must, of course, immediately be accompanied by the second: of himself man cannot see where his salvation lies; of himself he is not able to see that there is an ultimate basis for hope. And, of himself, man is not able to respond to this vision, i.e., of himself he is not able to hope. I realize how strange this idea is for people of this era. However, there is not much point in discussing it; it seems more meaningful to take note of it and consider the fact that this is what is handed down in the great tradition of the West: beginning with Plato—who knew it and said (for example, in the *Symposion*) that hope of finding one's way back to the soundness of the primordial form is linked to the presupposition of initiation—and continuing on to the proposition formulated in the Christian era: hope is a theological virtue. This means two things: first, that hope is not something like an "opinion," like a confident view of the world and of life; but hope is a virtue, a capacity in a person's existence, a rightness in his being; and second, this real capacity is a gift—in a very absolute sense; a person does not have it of himself. Therefore, we say, while healthy optimism is something we like and can also be helpful, it nevertheless says nothing about the real basis for hope. And to this extent the thesis of Camus is also open to misunderstanding (to say the least): whether life is worth living or not—that is perhaps a philosophical question; but this question cannot be answered in a philosophical way. The answer is theological—or there is no answer.

This does not mean that the real fulfilment in which all yearning is satisfied is something in the "world beyond," something separated from the place of real existence; something in which our present desires would not recognize themselves (so to speak). It is not unusual to think (and such an opinion is not surprising) that theology, as a whole, is concerned with things belonging to the world beyond; but this residue of the Enlightenment has nothing in common with the great Western theology, which—strangely!—hardly knows the distinction between this world and another world.

However, the fact remains: we are not yet in possession of what the inner unrest of our being needs for its peace. But "not yet having it" is more than "not having," and, of course, less than "having." It is precisely this "more" and this "less" that constitutes the essence of hope. This "not yet" makes up the innermost character of human existence itself which likewise contains the structural form of hope. Pascal expressed this in the paradoxical sentence: we are not, we hope to be!

This means: man is on a journey—in a much more radical sense than is usually meant in the now somewhat melodramatic talk about the pilgrimage of life. And this is a radical piece of wisdom in the Western tradition: hope is so essential to man that every attempt at pre-emption amounts to a distortion and a perversion. The ultimate satisfying of the need cannot be pre-empted. Presumptuousness, the word we use in reference to such a pre-emption, is wrongly associated with the Titans and the superhuman; it only applies to the inability to withstand the tension involved in hope within the structure of our existence. Despair is also a form of pre-emption; it is the anticipation of non-fulfilment. And despair also likes to deck itself out in heroic symbols in the frantic effort to contain the cries of pain within the inner self.

Both are non-human: the anticipation of disaster and the pre-emption of ultimate well-being. Both paralyze the flow of liberation which is in accord with the "not yet" character of the *viator*, a being whose existence implies hope.

But now, to return to our question: how do we go about living a life of hope? Here we are not referring to hoping for spring, not even hoping for what is normally called "happiness," not even hoping for peace in the world. But we mean hope of the ultimate, decisive, most profound satisfaction which can have no other name than "salvation." Nearer to the surface of our being there can be occasions of despair which are not of fundamental importance, just as, where there is real despair there can be occasions of hope which are also relatively insignificant. What has to happen for a person to have hope in the most fundamental sense? We have said it already: hope is a *gift*—in such an absolute sense that the individual cannot have it otherwise than as a gift, although he is able to accept or refuse the gift. That is no small thing.

The ancients have said that, above all, two things are necessary on man's part if he is to receive the gift of hope: high-mindedness and humility—two things which may seem mutually exclusive; on the one hand, that a person sees himself capable of great things and makes himself worthy of them, and on the other hand that at the same time he sees himself as creature.

But real hope remains a gift; as was clear in Platonic wisdom, it is only given to those initiated into the mysteries. But can one at least look in the direction from which this gift can be expected? Yes, that is possible. The direction is, by way of negation, given in the words of the New Testament: "If Christ did not rise, your hope is void."

Reflections on Prudence
(1952)

With words there can be decay and decline. It happens that words lose their original meaning and that they even come to have the opposite meaning. It is known that in the late Middle Ages a man with good manners would no longer use the word "Minne"—because its meaning had sunk to such a low and common level. Such changes are continually happening in every age; that is, in the sphere of language, the way of the world, so to speak—especially with regard to those words which have an ethical meaning and are therefore relevant to man. Words like hammer and rose scarcely change their meaning; but a person living in Goethe's era would not automatically understand our discussions about peace, guilt, or honor.

But what matters is that, nevertheless, certain basic notions remain recognizable in their original meaning—despite the continuous stream of changes of meaning in language. Precisely this is required of those who have to deal with words: to take care that reality and man's guide-lines can be adequately named. And how can that be managed? There is no recipe for it. Sometimes we will simply have to give up using a particular word. Who, today, wants to speak about "virtuous people"—although the reality meant by the words can still be encountered. Perhaps the word "virtue" itself is dead—it would almost seem so. Naturally, what is meant by "virtue" (that there is an extreme demand on a person which he has to meet—an extreme achievement in self-realization) must, in order not to lose its clear definition and its inspiring quality—and not to lose sight of the person's humanity—then be expressed in another way, ever anew.

I am not sure whether the word "prudence" should now be given up. "Why? The word is alive and in daily use in the spoken language!" That is true, whereas the word "virtue" hardly ever occurs in the contemporary vocabulary. But what does prudence mean? Who is prudent? A prudent person is the one who knows how to achieve his own advantage. (Do you think he will stand up for his convictions? No, he is too prudent for that—such is ordinary everyday language.) A prudent person is one who knows how to make sure that he does not run the risk of needing to be brave; a canny tactician who knows how to avoid personal commitment is prudent. The person who wants to avoid the moment of danger, the emergency, invokes prudence. — "Alright, where is this leading to? What would be wrong with defining the meaning of prudent as finding ways and means of not coming off too badly?" Now, considering that one of the fundamental human virtues was once called "prudence," I ask myself whether what used to be meant by this word is now at all recognizable amongst all the meanings which today we associate with the word. In current usage there is no bad deed which could not be called prudent and no good deed which could not be called imprudent. To tell the truth, for instance: can that not be imprudent? And the courageous person who goes out on a limb, is he not the stupid one? I don't know whether this use of language—and the way we speak is also always the way we think—does not always prevent us from seeing what is meant by the virtue of prudence. But what is meant by it? I was saying that "prudence" is the name given to "one" of the fundamental human virtues. A generation ago we learnt it off by heart at school: that prudence, justice, courage, and moderation are the four cardinal virtues. And so prudence is the first of them. It is seen not merely as the first, as the eldest—so to speak—of four sisters, but as the mother of the three others: the *genetrix virtutum*. That means (expressed less symbolically): only someone who is prudent can be just, courageous, and moderate. A person can be prudent and good only at the same time; prudence is part of the definition of a good action; there is no just or courageous action that could be called imprudent; and anyone who is unjust or cowardly is never prudent. Such formulations sound unusual, and it is hard to understand what is meant by them. (This is precisely what I am offering for consideration: we no longer know what prudence as a virtue means!) Then what does it mean? What is meant by saying that it is the mother of the virtues? The meaning is this: doing what is good presupposes knowledge of reality. Good can only be done by someone who knows the real state of affairs. It is not enough to have a "good intention." A further requirement is that one's gaze is directed at the reality of the real world and that the decision of the will—yes or no—is made dependent on one's knowledge of reality. An act is good if it is in accordance with things; and precisely this is what it means to be prudent: to let the situation, reality, dictate the course of action. Knowledge of the facts, what one has seen—to translate this into action is precisely the duty of prudence. "In our deeds and actions everything depends on the objects being grasped purely and treated according to their nature." These are the words of Goethe containing the kernel of the ancient teaching about the virtue of prudence—without naming it. Goethe sums it up in another statement. "All the rules of right behavior can be reduced to one: the truth."

All of this means (again): anyone who is not able to see things simply as they are, uninfluenced by the yes or no of the will; anyone who is not able to perceive, at first in silence, and then to convert what he sees and knows into a decision, is not in a position to do good, i.e., he is not capable of a good action in the full sense; he is not responsible and not mature.

But would that not mean that a person can only do good where a highly developed intelligence can be presupposed, that the ordinary person cannot be good in the full sense of the word—and is that not pure nonsense? Of course it is nonsense! And naturally that is not what is meant. — This is what is meant: no one can become a good person without possessing a certain kind of wisdom. It is the wisdom which the Middle Ages referred to, as did also Thomas à Kempis, saying: A man is wise if all things taste to him as they really are. For this, what is needed is not so much education and knowledge—if by knowledge one means direct self-awareness. A medieval *summa* says: "In that which pertains to prudence no one finds himself adequate in every way"—and therefore docility is part of prudence. This applies not just to ordinary people but to everyone. Docility is not just a quality of the so-called good pupil; it is the ability to let oneself be told something, which is a part of true open-mindedness. To be open in knowing and acknowledging that which is; simplicity in this sense is the core of the virtue of prudence. It is the simplicity of the eye spoken about in the New Testament:

If your eye is *simplex* then your whole body is in light—as it says in Matthew's gospel.

This simplicity of the prudent person, as a human attitude, is naturally not easy to achieve; it is even almost the seal of perfection. There is a surprising statement about this in teachings about life in the Middle Ages: the truly prudent person holds a middle course between two forms of wrong attitude: namely, between being too prudent on the one hand and being simply imprudent on the other. Perhaps one might say that this is not exactly a surprising thing to say. But the surprising element is not to be found here, but somewhat deeper—where there is a two-fold root from which it is said the two wrong attitudes originate. Plain imprudence (this has not to do with not knowing but with an attitude to things, to reality—a kind of lack of being alert, a lack of awareness)—this deficit has its root, according to the teaching of the High Middle Ages, in a lack of chastity. This word, too, has become endangered in many ways. It has perhaps become an impossible word. But we can pass over this. What this word means is that man has become lost amid the good things in the world of the senses: it not only weakens a person's capacity to make decisions but it also deprives the inner eye of its simplicity and focus.

The second kind deviation from prudence, an excessive prudence, is not a lack of alertness but an excessive watchfulness caught up in pure tension. Martin Luther called it cunning (Schalkheit), a name which, in his Bible translation, he uses in contradistinction to the openness, purity, and simplicity of the spirit. And this false prudence is, according to the opinion of the masters of the knightly period, rooted in avarice. This seems to me an astonishing thing to say. It means that the virtue of prudence, the attitude of objectivity in the observation and evaluation of things in reality, is opposed to avarice in a quite special way. Here "avarice" means more than a disordered love of money and possessions. Avarice means, as Gregory the Great expressed it, the immoderate striving after all the possessions through which a person thinks he can convince himself of his own greatness and importance. Avarice means here the anxious old-man syndrome of clutching at self-preservation, where there is only concern for security and affirmation. And by the way: the German language now seems vaguely to remember the hidden connection between avarice and false prudence. The Middle High German word "karg," which refers to the inventive cunning of selfishness, now belongs to the lexical field of prudence; and in Low German the miser is called a "Wiesen," a prudent man.

In between lack of chastity and avarice, in the sphere of self-preservation—which, however is selfless—rooted in a narrow strip of rich and precious soil, man's capacity to decide objectively can flourish. This ability, which in a very special sense is a human aptitude, is what the ancients called the virtue of prudence.

Conversation about Simplicity
(1951)

You were having some thoughts on the theme of "Simplicity as a virtue today." Did you come up with anything?

As usual, I proceeded like the priests at the Council of Trent who, as we know, had the Holy Scripture and the Works of St. Thomas on the table in front of them. And so I tried to find out what the concept "simplicity" meant in the teaching of the Bible and in classical Western theology.

I fear that the result might be a so very "supra-temporal" result that, while no one would doubt it, the spice of the "here and now" might be missing. The currently relevant.

That is true to some extent. But it is worth remembering that in this particular sphere the "currently relevant" does not mean much and that it is quite irrelevant what notions a private individual might produce. It is, for example, quite healthy to be told by Thomas Aquinas that it is very questionable to promote one particular virtue as if it were the most important of all, and that man, if he wants to be "right," must try to be "good," which always means to be all of these together: prudent, just, courageous, moderate.

This is exactly what I was afraid of: there is no reference here to the special historical situation, which also demands special virtues.

It will become clear that you are wrong. But let me first say that I, too, was surprised how little Thomas speaks about simplicity (*simplicitas*). Still, it is interesting that he almost equates it with genuineness. In Holy Scripture, by contrast, "simplicity" is almost a quintessence; a *vir simplex*, a "simple man": that is almost the same as a perfect man. Jacob is called this, and so is Job. "Simplicity of heart," "to live in simplicity," "the simplicity of the just man"—such formulations are to be found in great number both in the Old and the New Testament. Paul speaks (2 Corinthians 8, 2) of the "riches of simplicity." And, above all, in the words of the Lord Himself, the unfathomable statement: "If your eye is simple your whole body is in the light" (Matthew 6:22 and Luke 11:34).

But does *simplicitas* here not mean being straight, pure, natural, humble? And we mean something quite different when we demand simplicity.

I admit that we do mean something quite particular; but I think we should be careful not to separate our ideal of simplicity from this broader and richer semantic field. What would be the point and, above all, what weight would such a demand for simplicity have if it did not include that we should in our hearts be pure, humble, straight, simple, open, with nothing false in us, upright, not artificial, and true?

All of that has timeless value, which I do not dispute. Yet, when we speak of simplicity we have in mind something which, for the young person, is of "special" importance, i.e., a distinct importance which is not always valid in the same way. You don't seem to see that.

Not so! Of course, we are not as unique as we sometimes think we are. For example, the Stoa of late antiquity spoke about simplicity in the same vein as "we" do;

Seneca and Marcus Aurelius praise the undemanding life of the modest man living in the midst of a society characterized by an excess of possibilities for pleasure and at the same time great insecurity and disorder in the social and political spheres. In such times simplicity is seen as the only way to achieve an inner stance, calm, ascendancy, independence, peace, which, of course, can only happen if this attitude remains free of resentment, self-deception, and sour grapes—sour because they hang from too high a branch; in a word, when all the elements are realized which are meant by the undiminished concept of *simplicitas*. It is not possible to satisfy a "need of our time" if we lose sight of what has "timeless value."

But you would agree that simplicity of that particular kind—let's sum it up as "Doing without luxury"—really is a virtue which is required of young people in this era and in this sense is appropriate to our times?

Yes, I agree. Being up-to-date is not that which directly fits in with current taste but which responds to the forces driving the future. It is possible to respond either with a yes or a no.

I can see where this is leading. You would see the ideal of simplicity as a negative answer to this world of ours, in which ever new needs are awakened which are, it is true, artificial but nevertheless so real that they demand satisfaction—in food and drink, in fashionable clothing, in "entertainment" (cinema, radio, periodicals, television), in the most ephemeral pleasures (cocktails, cigarettes)—and so forth. That is obvious. It is all around us.

And yet this is only one side of the coin. The other side seems to me almost more important—if it is perhaps not so "easy to understand." In our era there is also a false ideal of simplicity and it looks as if it is becoming steadily more accepted. I am referring to that "proletarian" view of life according to which everything appears as "irresponsible luxury" that does not serve "increase in production," "fulfilment of the plan," "social progress," and "the common good" (in the economic sense).

And so it would seem important from two angles to understand and promote simplicity as a virtue precisely of our generation. — But it is not clear to me how that is an answer to the ideal of the "proletarian." What is this answer?

The answer is that true human richness does not consist in the satisfaction of hunger although this an essential need in life; that also the non-useful is necessary: beauty, superfluity, fullness; that the grey bareness and sparseness of the functionary's life as such is inhuman.

That is doubtless correct. But what does that have to do with the ideal of simplicity? In this you seem to be arguing against yourself.

As I said, this is rather complicated. The "proletarian" ideal did not, I believe, gain such influence by chance. It seems to be an anticipation of part of our future. The cultural impoverishment of man is indeed progressing. What is necessary now is that we inwardly prepare ourselves to accept this poverty and at the same time not give up the true and genuine human riches. And precisely this should be discussed in the demand for true simplicity.

And so you would now modify your no to "luxury" to some extent?

No, by no means. On the contrary, I believe that the true wealth of man is endangered more by "comfort" than by proletarian frugality. In Gertrud von le Fort's book about women we find the astonishing words: "Not the face of the bolshevist proletarian, distorted by hunger and hatred, is the true expression of modern godlessness, but the woman who is dedicated to the most pitiful of all cults—that of her own body." Here the root of a selfish luxurious existence is laid bare to its metaphysical roots. And anyone who wants to speak adequately about the right kind of simplicity must go down into these depths where it becomes clear that, as the biblical concept of *simplicitas* says, simplicity is ultimately a religious attitude. This will enable us to decide about the how, the what, the how much and the how little; it will be possible, but also necessary.

Chivalry as a Soldier's Stance (1942)

1

In time of war it can happen that every conceivable human perfection is attributed to the soldier as belonging to his essence. This means not just courage and a spirit of aggression, but also, for example, a sense of humor is vaunted as a "soldierly" virtue. Such attributions are based on the deeply rooted idea that only a whole and genuine person can be a good soldier. This idea is behind the eight "duties of the German soldier" which undertake to outline an almost complete and closed ethical image of man and go far beyond the sphere of the military in the narrowest sense. In this they are clearly distinct from the "articles of war" of previous ages.

It is nevertheless possible to draw a clear distinction between those soldierly virtues derived directly from the most particular functions of a soldier, namely the commitment to fight, and those other virtues, the validity of which is more broadly based. On the one hand there are, for example, courage, fighting spirit, commitment, resistance; and on the other hand there is, for example, "godliness," which is spoken about in the "Duties of the German Soldier."

This distinction is not merely of theoretical consequence. It concerns two radically opposed sets of values for a soldier. One of them is bolshevist. The other could be referred to as "Western" because it lives from all the historical energies which have shaped the West as a spiritual reality.

According to the bolshevist idea, the good soldier is one who has suitability for military tasks and follows orders in performing this function. Everything which limits this bare suitability for the task, but also only that, is not soldierly. Personal values of a human character which are not directly connected with the military function are of no consequence. They may even be suspect. The concept of an "Army Ethic" is, in the sphere of bolshevist thinking about soldiering, unthinkable. In this context, "Army Ethic" equals regulations; and only what is against regulations is unsoldierly. The bolshevist criterion is: complete identification with the team operating the machinery of war. The reduction of the person to being a cog in the wheel, which is characteristic of bolshevism as a whole, is seen here where it is applied to the military sphere.

Anyone who is thinking within the Western tradition will balk at using the word "soldier" in this context. He would find it more correct to speak of a military execution functionary. We need to be clear that anyone who takes his counter arguments solely from the narrow military sphere will in no way be able to produce a convincing criticism of the bolshevist view of soldiery. It is not possible, for example, to base the need for religious commitment on the argument that soldiers who are believers are "better able to cope with dying." That would logically be an inversion of the true order of things and a hopeless educational task—quite apart from the fact that its foundation in reality is questionable: the idea of an "heroic downfall" for its own sake has its origin in nihilism, not in religion.

The crucial point is this: the Western view of soldiery is precisely not the mere projection of military needs onto the plane of humanity in general or of morality; rather, it expresses the claim that an ethical conception of man in accordance with the total essence of man and reality has validity also in the military sphere. Only on this basis can the idea of "soldier" be defended logically and meaningfully against that of the "military execution functionary."

2

Through this clarification we can see that chivalry as a "soldierly attitude" cannot be based on the purely military function, although precisely chivalry in a quite special sense, more than, for instance, "godliness," is a virtue which specifically befits the soldier. Purely military function is conceivable without chivalry; but: "ethically justified soldiery is never present where there is no chivalry" (Simoneit).

What is chivalry? It is the attitude, firstly, of a man who exercises power and who has superior power. It is the attitude, secondly, which always has another person in view, and indeed one who is inferior with regard to power and who, despite the exterior inferiority, is acknowledged as of equal rank. This last point is important: chivalry is not just caring and not just sparing. It is conceivable that a person who has superior power is protective, as when one protects an animal from starving to death, or that one spares someone without deigning to look at the person who escapes with his life. Chivalry includes the idea that the person who is inferior in power can be addressed and appreciated as not at all inferior in other respects, perhaps even as superior.

Chivalry is the attitude of the strong in relation to the defenseless and the weak, who, in their vulnerability, are confirmed as not less worthy of armed protection than the strong. And they are to be protected by the strong. In all traditional laws of chivalry care for "widows and orphans" has pride of place. Chivalry is especially called on when these defenseless people are suffering injustice and violence. "To fight a duel to rescue every innocent person"— that is solemnly announced in the text of an accolade from the year 1247 as the most important "rule of chivalry."

Chivalry is the attitude of a man towards a woman insofar as she is seen as the weaker and yet is respected and honored as equal or even of higher rank. It is interesting to note that chivalry as an ideal in social intercourse of the sexes fades according as the contrast, which is a presupposition of chivalry, disappears from the general consciousness.

Chivalry is, above all, the attitude of the stronger opponent towards the weaker, who, again, in this weaker position is explicitly acknowledged and confirmed as equal—as an equally brave fighter or as belonging to the same civilized circle or, finally, sharing in the same human dignity.

Wherever a person who exercises power, in the face of one who is inferior to him in power and is in his power, has in common with him the same dignity—even if only that they share the name of human beings—there the model of chivalry raises its claim. There is no need for further explanation of how much this claim precisely concerns the soldier and his duty, and how much chivalry is a "soldierly attitude."

3

Historically we see chivalry in a two-fold form: as a properly ethical norm and, socially, as one of the rules of the game.

The latter, which usually has its roots in the former, usually has its validity from being linked to particular social classes and to particular periods. The codex of chivalrous behavior, not only in the courtly and erotic spheres but also in war, has undergone considerable change. There was, for example, a time where it was considered unchivalrous in the highest degree to attack the opposing army in battle if it had not yet mustered for combat.

To imitate and to adopt rules of the game for chivalry from other ages or other countries because of their imposing display or historical fame is an undertaking doomed to failure on account of its own incompatibility with history. New forms and rules of the game are only born out of the ethical model of chivalry. This transcends time as does the human mind itself. Its historical fruitfulness will not cease as long as we see as valid the interpretations and evaluations which are included in this model like premises in a conclusion and which concern the world as a whole—interpretations and evaluations which are more or less expressly known and affirmed. Just as all obligation is founded in being, so all models of behavior are rooted in the knowledge of reality. In the same way, false aspirations and spurious ideals grow, of necessity, out of non-real or inadequate interpretations of the world of being.

4

Some fundamental statements—as interpretations of the world to which the ethical ideal of chivalry refers back and which are expressed in it—may be given here in summary form.

First: the inner core realities and values of human life are, from their very foundation, both powerless and yet possessing sovereign power. They can, by purely external power, be destroyed or inhibited in their development, but they can never be built up or strengthened through positive influence from within. The chivalrous person bows to this metaphysical situation. By acknowledging the loser he acknowledges that his own power is limited. He confirms that it is ultimately nothing.

Second: External power is legitimated—not exclusively, but also not in the last instance—by protecting those things which of themselves have no power, enabling them to grow and develop according to their own inner laws. In this case, as I have already said, the powerful element is not essentially the giving part.

Third: In Wolfram's "Parzival," Gurnemanz summarizes the meaning of the rules for knights: "You have an elevated life, and it becomes loftier if your will remains such that you have mercy on the army of the oppressed"; "show that you follow my teaching by exercising mercy as well as bravery in battle!" And of Parzival himself is said: "Then the victor soon thought of Gurnemanz's teaching, that a brave man should always be prepared to be merciful." For a modern person it is difficult to distinguish Wolfram's concept of "mercy" from the concept of "sympathy" as it developed in the second half of the nineteenth century and, for example, was formulated in the fight against vivisections and similar phenomena. This kind of "sympathy," which was rightly attacked by Nietzsche, is closer to nerviness than to an intellectual ethical attitude. But "mercy" originates not from the physical incapability of looking at another's suffering but from the free decision of the powerful person who magnanimously sets himself limits and honors the dignity of the vanquished as greater than power. This, therefore, is the third fundamental idea on which the ethical idea "mercy" is based. It is not to be seen as an act of weakness but as a particularly lofty exercise of power. In medieval texts mercy is referred to as the "fullness of justice" (plenitude justitiae); but exercising justice is the natural role of the powerful. And it is said of the omnipotence of God that it is revealed first by His mercy.

It is in the climate of such basic conceptions that the ideal of chivalry grew.

5

No matter to what extent physical courage and a dare-devil attitude are required for engagement in battle, only moral courage rooted in the inner core of the ethical person can, in the long run, rise to the challenge of an extremely serious situation. Moral courage—that is, in general terms, the inner willingness, for the sake of justice, to accept wounds and even death in attack and resistance in the cause of justice.

As the old classical saying has it: every virtue is always intrinsically connected with all the others, so that there can be no bravery without truth, justice, discipline. It is a bourgeois illusion to think that a person can be just without being exposed to the necessity to show courage. It is no less a perversion of sense to think that a person can be brave if fighting on the side of injustice; courage of the criminal is nonsense. Equally, courage as a moral virtue can have nothing to do with licentiousness. In "Parzival" we read: "I never heard of a man being praised for licentious bravery."

But chivalry includes the idea that the exercise of power does not lose itself in intoxication with power; that the human dignity also of the defenseless is respected; that opposition does not turn into personal hatred; that the strong person controls himself and sets boundaries for himself.

And so, wherever brave commitment is ennobled by chivalry a guarantee is given that courage springs from the same depths of the person from which the great ethical decisions which determine our lives are born. Therefore, chivalry is, accordingly, the touchstone of morally genuine courage. And in this it shows itself as a "soldierly" attitude in a still deeper sense.

What Each One of Us Should Do
(New Year's Eve 1951)

How does a private person—one who has no public remit, whether from church or state—want to say what each of us should do! "Interesting"—yes, it could perhaps be interesting to hear what Mr X, whose book one may have read, has to say in answer to the question: "What, in your opinion, should every one of us do?" But interest of this kind, the merely interesting, is not worth the trouble. On the other hand it is very much worthwhile to ponder for a moment where such information as we are looking for here is to be found. How do we find out, once and for all, what people should do? Who decides about that? I think not a little would be achieved if, pondering the question seriously, one arrived at the answer: in truth, what we should do—that is a theme about which one should not lightly express some opinion or other or listen to such opinions. We are not at all concerned with clever notions; and mere reflection and close concentration are also not adequate. But? In order to come up with something of consequence one would need already to have access—in the strictest sense of the word—to supra-human wisdom. Such wisdom is by no means inaccessible. It is expressly promulgated and revealed, even though, on the other hand, it is not of easy access to ordinary everyday levels of thought. It is, so to speak, not available without cost.

An "individual" person might be able simply to translate into everyday language something of that supra-individual wisdom, knowing full well and making no secret of the fact that his attempt cannot be fully successful. He might do this without any authority and without any claim to subjective originality, and he may succeed in being heard where the listener's focus is not solely on what is "interesting."

Fine. But is it necessary to go straight to abstract questions of principle? We Germans, at New Year's eve 1951/52, are bogged down with a thousand highly concrete questions which are unanswered and undecided—socialization, militarization, pan-German elections! Tell me, what should happen? How is the individual to decide? — It may be deeply disappointing, but I am not prepared to take on these questions posed in this way. It is not for me to say, in these areas, "what each one of us should do."

Nevertheless, no one will in all seriousness say that that traditional wisdom (about what people should do) does not equally and very definitely concern the very concrete questions of our era—even the political questions. If we ask: "What should each one of us do?" we must also ask the further question: "... do, to achieve what?" Everyday thinking has almost become accustomed to add: "... do, against what?" If the answer were to be: against the disorder in the world; or, positively: to have us live more humanly (i.e., more meaningfully, rightly—or, and it comes to the same thing, more according to what is divine in man), such an approach could not be called abstract. Of course, it is still possible to fall very easily into the abstract, into the sphere of the velleity, the utopian, into the realm of Mr. Utinam (utinam: "Would that ..."—which we learnt in studying Latin at school. As students we often flung the expression at one another in ironic and mocking tones if someone, with his suggestions and plans, had strayed too far into the unreal). "If only people would follow the Ten Commandments!" "If only Europe would become Christian!"—that is an abstract answer, an abstractly correct answer, by the way; but it is still a pure *"would that"* answer—i.e., it is no answer at all to the question about what is to be done. If, on the other hand, every individual were to stand up and say: "Before you do anything you must be silent and listen, otherwise you spoil your deed from the beginning; if you do not see the reality, things the way they are, you cannot act properly towards other individuals in society as a whole; be prepared for the fact that the true and the good are not achieved without effort, but that you have to commit to them (you cannot expect it to be otherwise: this is the way the world is structured); do not love your life so much that you lose it, i.e., that you do not let your desire for pleasure (and there is nothing to be said against it) grow so far out of control that, in the end, you are incapable of seeing reality as it is and of doing what is right and of standing up for it"—if every individual were to speak like this he would have done nothing but formulate, in his own way, the age-old wisdom contained in the four cardinal virtues of prudence, justice, courage, and moderation; but, it seems to me, he would have given a rather concrete answer to the question about what each one of us should do. Who could maintain that the reality of human life we meet every day is not recognizable here? This can be conceded. But Plato, too, could have spoken to his contemporaries in this vein! — That is true. But would his statement not also have been quite concrete also in those days?

Nevertheless, there is such a thing as history! Each epoch is characterized by its own particular necessities—even within the same general ethical sphere. Perhaps we can put it like this: each age tends to suppress and forget particular elements of the eternally valid truth which, by its very nature, should always be realized. This is what defines the particular duty of precisely this time, and thus the question of what each of us—currently living, of course—should do must be answered in a particular, distinct way. This is precisely the answer we are looking for! What is necessary today? There is much to suggest that the same is required of a person today as was always and will always be required. And yet perhaps it can still be said what a person should do, precisely in our time. One ought, for example, learn to listen again. I do not mean obeying (there seems to be no lack of this); what is meant is exactness, dependability, objectivity of listening; simply that something that is heard, read, or seen is properly grasped—without distortion or diminution. When we hear two different people relating the same simple fact, when we read book reviews, when we follow political debates, the ability to know what exactly happened, was said or was written seems to be dying out! But it is clear that here we are concerned with a simple fundamental ability—a presupposition for justice—with the basis on which human life is lived: to be open to the truth of things in the real world and to act according to one's grasp of the truth.

I believe, in fact, that it is possible to do something so that this ability to listen does not degenerate further—even that it can be restored and even perfected; "each one of us" can (and therefore should) do something about it.

In scholastic disputation which, for several centuries in the West was the most disciplined and polished form of debate ever developed, the fundamental rule was that the defendant, before he was allowed to answer, had to repeat the opponent's argument and receive his assurance that he had it right. It cannot be imagined how the introduction of such a rule would mean for the purification of the political atmosphere in Germany. — No, it is not imaginable—and thus it is a rather clear case of "utinam," "would that," utopia! — I contest this! Everyone is put in the situation every day where he can practice listening; one can teach it to children, one's own children, and one's pupils. One can object to obviously faulty listening, in public one can at least withhold applause; someone who is indiscriminately abusive can be met with a dismissive look which drives away slanderous speech like clouds before the North wind (this image is to be found, I believe, in the Old Testament); above all, to say it again, we should learn to listen ourselves! This is something which I truly believe each of us should do! (That in this way we could come to hear something quite different is another story!)

There is something further to mention which people precisely in our era should consider. Of course, it is questionable whether pondering, thinking, contemplating can at all be considered as "doing." But if Heraclitus referred to sleepers as active and as collaborators in the events around us—and some comments would be in order here—how much more would the person actively knowing and contemplating the truth and perceiving reality be seen as an active person, as one who does something!

And so, the question about what each one of us should do to bring about a perfect situation in the world ... The answer could be: the most effective political slogans of our age owe their advertising power to this notion: that the fruit of their influence will be a perfect world. What are we to think of this? We are to see that this absolute claim is inhuman and that it is this claim that almost with necessity gives to our actions that inhuman mindlessness which is such a familiar part of our experience. We are not the master of world history; its blueprint is not accessible to us. We realize the plan by doing what is necessary in a given situation. Precisely this fragmentary aspect, the lack of finality, the improvised and, so to speak, the patching aspect is the human part of all history—"human" not in the sense of inadequacy but rather in the sense of "not inhuman." And so anyone who asks what each of us should do will have to keep in mind this deeper meaning and the accompanying threat. Of course, misgivings are not the end of it. How would it be if people in this age were to have lost confidence in the fragmentary nature of our history?

Yet again our discussion runs up against its limits— which I have decided at this point not to cross. But a final word is necessary: beyond the boundary lies another sphere in which the question: "What should each one of us do?" takes on a completely new meaning, in the face of which our attempt at an answer would prove to be rather inconsequential.

On Private Property
(1950)

Thomas Aquinas, Summa theologica [II, II, 66, 2]: "With regard to external things man has two possibilities. One is the power of providing and disposing. And in this regard man is allowed to have property. There are three reasons why this is necessary for human life. First, because everyone puts more effort into looking after what belongs to him alone than to what belongs to all or many in common; everyone shuns the effort and leaves it to others to look after what is common to all—as is seen where there are many servants. Second, because human affairs are handled in a more orderly way when individuals are given their own responsibility for a particular thing, whereas it would have to lead to disorder if everyone, without distinction, had to deal with everything. Third, because peaceful relations between people are best maintained when each one is content with what he has himself; we see that amongst those who possess things in common and without distinction quarrels more frequently occur.

The other possibility for man with regard to external things is using them. In this respect man cannot possess external things as his own but as things owned in common so that he can distribute them when others are in need. Thus the apostle says: "Tell the rich of this world to give easily, to communicate to others, etc." (1 Timothy 6, 17)

Objection: "It seems it is not permitted to possess something as one's own, for everything that is against natural law is not allowed. But according to natural law everything is owned jointly. This mutuality is contrary to individual possession, and therefore it is not permitted that anyone takes any external thing as his own."

Answer: "The common aspect of goods is ascribed to natural law not in such a way that natural law requires that all goods be owned jointly and nothing could be owned privately, but because the division of possessions takes place not on the basis of natural law but rather according to human arrangement, which belongs to positive law. For this reason personal ownership is not against natural law but is added to natural law as an accomplishment of human reason."

Let us suppose that a modern communist or socialist, a man of sound good sense and by no means unintelligent but also not familiar with the scientific distinctions between possession, property, custom, right of use—let us suppose that such a man were to read in our text the words of St. Thomas: it must be said that the commonality of goods is ascribed to natural law. Probably he would be quite pleased with this sentence; he would see it as a confirmation of modern collectivism or at least as approval of the institution of collective ownership.

Let us suppose, furthermore, that a modern liberal, an individualist for whom the private property arrangement has an inviolable, even "sacred" character, and who is also a man of sound good sense, but not acquainted with the distinctions found in academic social philosophy—let us suppose that this man would answer the communist, saying: "No, your interpretation is clearly wrong. That cannot really be St. Thomas's opinion. I am reading in the same article the following sentence: 'It is permitted to man to have property, and it is even necessary for human life.'"

Both are quoting real sentences from St. Thomas which seem to contradict one another. Each brings forward a sentence which must be a stumbling block, a thorn in the side to the other. Each of them thinks that the two positions are incompatible. The question is: in what sense, in what way can they be compatible?

I will attempt, by somewhat presumptuously playing the part of St. Thomas for a moment, briefly to answer this question for both parties who contradict not only one another but also St. Thomas.

I am turning first to the communist, and I maintain that the sentence according to which the commonality of goods corresponds to natural law contains neither a confirmation nor a negation of collective property and neither a confirmation nor a negation of private property. The communist will probably interrupt me sharply: "I am reading here expressly commonality of goods. Then who is the owner?" — Thomas would, I think, answer: "The community is the owner—if the sentence did not mean this the words would have no meaning. They would just be a manner of speaking. You are right: the subject, the bearer of the right to ownership of the goods of the world is really, according to natural law, the community. But: this 'community' does not mean the state or the municipality or the party or any kind of concrete social group." — "Then who is the subject and bearer; who is the owner— if I am correct in speaking of a commonality of goods?"

The answer will have to be: the subject, the owner is "man" as such (as this is meant in the sentence "Let us make man ..."); the subject is, so to speak, Adam, understood as the origin and the totality of all human reality.

"Man" in this sense certainly refers to the community; it means humanity as a whole. "Man" in this sense is the subject of the right to ownership of non-spiritual creation, and in this both sides are seen as a totality; as yet there is no kind of division or individuation. And *this* kind of ownership corresponds to natural law—which means that this right to ownership stems directly both from the nature of man and from the nature of non-spiritual reality.

Perhaps this outcome seems at first sight nothing particularly exciting, something quite obvious. And it is indeed part of the concept of natural law that its content is something straightforwardly "natural"; something that is obvious in itself. But this has consequences which are not at all obvious to everybody.

The communist will perhaps say: "I am curious to see how you come from the starting position 'commonality of goods' to the conclusion that a system of private property is the best system. How can it be possible, from such a conclusion, to see any kind of commonality of goods?" I would answer: "You will most certainly be in a position to recognize this principle in that conclusion, which, by the way, is not the slightest confirmation of the 'sacredness' of private property."

But first some more detail about the meaning of the "principle" just formulated. The inner meaning of ownership is this: things of a lower order serve to sustain human life (what is meant here is the totality of human life). That means that the meaning and aim of human ownership with regard to the non-spiritual world is, according to natural law, that humanity as a whole, without any exception, is enabled to use the goods in the world for a truly *res inferiores sunt ordinatae ad hoc, quod ex his subveniatur hominum necessitati* human life. And the question is in what way this general, deep and unique sense of belonging, possessing, owning—directly given with the nature of man and of things—can be realized.

By asking this question we find ourselves no longer on the level of principles and goals; we are on the level of "ways and means." And this is the level on which concepts such as common property and private property are up for discussion. Both are secondary and subordinate. Neither private property nor common property are directly related to natural law; neither private property nor common property are in contradiction with natural law.

And yet, a liberal individualist might say with some sense of satisfaction, "Thomas ultimately comes to the conclusion that private property is a necessity." And "therefore," the communist will add, "he has thus made the principle of the commonality of goods disappear."

I admit that Thomas does, in fact, support the idea of private property. He has three reasons: an economic reason (better output from work), a social reason (better organization of the community), and a political reason (easier preservation of peace). But this does not in the least mean that Thomas would accept the liberal conception of the "sacredness" of private property. Here we have to speak of severe limitations which show that the aim of the private property system is indeed the original "commonality of goods" which has its validity from natural law.

First, all private property is encumbered with a "social mortgage"; i.e., the owner, in using his property, has to consider the needs of his neighbour; he must, as our text says, "be prepared to share with others when they are in need." It is possible that here the liberal, perhaps rather too hurriedly, expresses his agreement while thinking (perhaps): "The only crucial point is, who has legal control; then we are prepared to take on that 'mortgage'." And the communist will perhaps say: "In this way the 'commonality of goods' becomes a question of private charitable activity." Thomas would, on the contrary, again assert very strongly that the duty to "share with others who are in need" is a duty based not only on love but on justice.

But it is much more important that Thomas would say: the arguments in favor of private property belong to the sphere of ways and means; i.e., their strength derives from the private property system really being a means to achieve the end: that "man" as a whole is put in a position to lead a truly human life (insofar as possession of the goods of this world can be of assistance in this). If this goal, which is primarily and directly bound up with the natural law, were to be positively endangered or even thwarted, the means—private property—would have to be adjusted and changed; perhaps it would *eo ipso* be suspended. It is indeed totally suspended in the case of extreme need: a person who, in danger of dying of hunger, takes something belonging to another is, in reality, not taking away another's property: he is taking his own property, something that belongs to him (*per talem necessitatem efficitur suum*). In this case the original commonality of goods re-establishes itself. With regard to it, private property is only a means.

Further: the system of private property can be modified if achieving the prior right in natural law—the "commonality of goods"—be in principle endangered. Thus the Encyclical *Quadragesimo Anno* in no way contradicts the teaching of St. Thomas. It calls on him explicitly in saying that under certain circumstances one can quite justifiably demand that certain kinds of goods should be reserved for public ownership. This does not contradict Thomas's defense of private property, because the defense is not unconditional, but precisely conditional. This is the condition: the realization of the natural and proper sense of all property, so that humanity as a whole is enabled, and will remain enabled, to use the goods of this world to make a truly human existence possible.

A Short Note on Thomas Aquinas (1951)

In the works of St. Thomas, who is called the Common Doctor, the philosophical tradition of Greece is combined with the theological wisdom of the first Christian centuries. The basis of this combination is the spirituality shaped by Holy Scripture and the sacramental life of the Church. The result is an admirable structural framework which is "closed," but which nevertheless explicitly allows room for the mystery of being and the reverential silence it inspires. The Church has given Thomas a rank conceded to no other Doctor of the Church. The Thomas encyclical of Pius XI ["Studiorum ducem" 29.6.1923] says that the Church shows in every way that it has made his teaching her own. On the other hand, the same encyclical gives a warning against a pedantic and sterile canonizing of St. Thomas, something which would be entirely opposed to his way of thinking.

Thomas was born in 1225 in Roccasicca, in the Province of Naples; he comes from a Langobard-Norman family; his father belonged to the court nobility of the Hohenstaufen Emperor Frederick II. Thomas spent his childhood years in Monte Cassino. In 1239 he came to Naples and studied at the University of Frederick II which shortly beforehand had been founded as the first purely state university of the West. In Naples he had two decisive encounters: with the mendicant order movement and with Aristotle. The first encounter led to his joining the Dominican Order [1244]; the second, brought about by an Irishman teaching at the University, became the first step towards the incorporation of Aristotelian wisdom into the theological and philosophical structure of the Christian Weltanschauung.

In 1245 Thomas came to Paris, where he met Albertus Magnus, with whom, a little later, he went to Cologne for a few years (1248–1252); then he was appointed Professor of Theology, teaching publicly at the University of Paris from 1256 to 1259. From then onwards, Thomas, whose life is sometimes portrayed as particularly uneventful, was never longer than two or three years in the same place and in the same post. Charged with setting up Dominican schools, teaching at the Papal court of Urban IV and Clement IV, he then had a second, extremely fruitful time lecturing at the Paris University. This work took its toll on him and undermined his strength, so that on the way to fulfilling his last duty (participation in the Council of Lyon) he died, not yet fifty years old, in the Cistercian monastery Fossanuova in southern Italy (1274). He was canonized in 1323, and in 1367 he was made Doctor of the Church.

His writings—apart from a great number of smaller polemical pamphlets (mostly in defense of the mendicant orders), and essays dealing with philosophy, dogma and asceticism—comprised comprehensive commentaries on nearly all the works of Aristotle but also on several books of Sacred Scripture (the gospels of Matthew and John and the Letters of St. Paul); on Peter Lombard's book of Sentences compiled from the works of the Fathers of the Church, especially Augustine. We need also to mention the *Quaestiones* works about Truth, the Virtues, Evil, the power of God, and also, finally, both of the Summae: the summa against the heathens and the Theological Summa (which, of course, remained a fragment—not because Thomas died in the throes of writing it, but because, as a result of a mystical experience in the late autumn of 1273, he refused to continue writing: "All that I have written seems to me like chaff compared with what I have seen and what has been revealed to me").

One can perhaps say that the most profound influence Thomas had on his time was through his Aristotle commentaries; that the *Quaestiones* contained the most profound developments of his own particular problems; and that the strongest and most direct influences on later centuries came from the *Summa theologica*, which he himself saw as a handbook for beginners.

The personality of St. Thomas is decisively shaped by the purity and passion of his relationship to truth. This explains his dedication as a teacher, committed to absorbing reality as it is, grasping it with complete fidelity and unquenchable thirst, and to making this store of knowledge—in an ingenious and simple order—easily accessible to the understanding even of beginners.

Although his world view is so rich and, as I said at the beginning, comprises so many different elements combining to form a striking unity that can neither simply be characterized as "Aristotelianism" or any other "ism" (above all, the Neoplatonist element which seems irreconcilable with Aristotle is important here: there are more than 1700 quotations from the works of Dionysius the Areopagite!)—yet his turning to Aristotle is what gives his work its decisive character. Thus it is especially important for an understanding of the "Common Doctor" that we grasp this clearly. It is a decisive fact, first of all, that Thomas did not bring, from Aristotle, into his Christian understanding of being, anything alien, heathen, or "Greek," but that in this natural wisdom about the world which was for ages to be found in Christendom (for example, in Justin, Clement of Alexandria, and others) he "recognized" the affirmation of the visible world of creation which was formulated there as a theological issue. With this affirmation of the natural sense world (even within man himself, understood as an essentially physical being) Thomas opposes, on the one hand, the "unworldliness" of the medieval Augustine, but also, on the other hand, the so-called "Latin Averroism" (a form of Aristotelianism which was influenced by Arabian philosophy and which paved the way for the separation of culture from the theological sphere). St. Thomas's orientation towards reality has expressly religious and theological roots: not only would it be "contempt for the Creator of nature to say that the affirmation of nature is not right," but also the sacraments ("that man is given the medicine of salvation precisely in visible things") are proof of the ontological goodness of the visible world of senses.

Thomas's incorporation of the "world" into the Christian interpretation of reality and into the Christian attitude, for the first time with systematic logic, is a process in which what is specifically Western takes shape. And the opponents of St. Thomas at the time show today the dangers facing the Western mind: on the one hand, the spiritualistic and supernaturalistic turning aside from creative reality, and, on the other hand, secularization in all its forms and guises.

Thomas Aquinas as Teacher
(1949)

In his works, St. Thomas did not speak of himself; he did not characterize himself. It is known that Augustine said of himself that he was one of those who "write as they grow, and grow as they write." Augustine said of himself that he was essentially a writer; Theodor Haecker sees in his formulation a kind of definition of the writer. Naturally the question remains whether one has really grasped the essence of St. Augustine when one sees him as a "writer"; but answering this question is not our present task.

I believe, however, that if, instead of saying "writer" one were to say "teacher," one would have grasped an essential characteristic of St. Thomas; if we say that Thomas belongs to those who teach as they grow, and grow as they teach, then Thomas was essentially a teacher. This is, as Gilson has said, the most enduring aspect of St. Thomas's personality: "The saint was essentially a teacher of the Church; the man was a teacher of theology and philosophy; and also the mystic never separated his meditations from the instruction which was perhaps enkindled by them."

According to Thomas, teaching is one of the highest and most perfect forms of intellectual life, because in teaching both of the fundamental forms of human existence—the vita contemplativa and the vita activa—are linked to one another, and this not by way of any artificial combination and purely factual proximity but by way of an organic, natural connection based on intrinsic necessity. Anyone who is teaching in the genuine sense, hands on a truth—grasped in pure, receptive attention—to persons who, listening, want to and ought to receive this truth. The teacher looks at the truth of things—that is the contemplative aspect of teaching; it is the silent aspect, the listening in silence, without which the word of the teacher would have no provenance. It would be talk, posturing, chat, deceit. The teacher keeps his listeners in mind (not just the truth of things); he submits himself to the methodically disciplined, arduous work of interpretation, of presenting, of mediating—that is the element of vita activa in teaching. It is the fruitful aspect which is not already included in contemplation as a part of it. Thus, according to Thomas in the Summa theologica, the activity of teaching, in which the vita contemplativa and the vita activa are combined, is of a higher order than pure contemplation— as long as we are dealing with genuine teaching which is derived ex plenitudine contemplationis. Then teaching is something greater than contemplation alone: "just as enlightening is something greater than throwing light" (sicut ... majus est illuminare quam lucere).

A person is all the more a teacher the more intensely and passionately both of these aspects are lived out: the relationship to truth, the power of silent grasping of reality on the one hand and, on the other hand, the loving attention to the listeners who are to be led by the teacher in such a way that they too will see the truth of things. We can now say that Thomas realized both, with extreme intensity; so much so that his innermost self seems to be defined and shaped by it.

When Thomas entered the Dominican order, the Dominicans in Naples were very quick to send away this young man who had important imperial and family connections; he was immediately on his way to Paris. It is well known that Thomas's rise to his future fame was not without effort. Instead, his own brothers intercepted him on the way and summarily locked him up in a castle belonging to his father, San Giovanni, where Thomas remained for a year in captivity—without, of course, wavering in his decision to belong to the Order of Preachers. During this time something happened that was reported as the "girding by an angel"; an event which, as we can read in the earliest, almost contemporary biography by Wilhelm von Tocco, Thomas himself, towards the end of his life, related to his friend, secretary, and travel companion Reginald von Piperno. We can accept this story or dismiss it as legend, in which case there would be no further debate. But in any case it would, in my opinion, be painfully inappropriate to attempt a psychoanalytical commentary.

The story can quickly be told: the robust importunateness of the brothers of young Thomas, who attempted in every way to make him change his mind, went so far that one day they brought their prisoner a dolled-up courtesan. Now Thomas immediately showed the girl the door, quite without ceremony. But it seems that the 19- to 20-year-old went through, in these moments, a tremendously violent inner struggle. According to Wilhelm von Tocco, Thomas immediately afterwards collapsed at the threshold of his room and, exhausted, fell into a deep sleep. He awoke out of this sleep with a loud cry; he had cried out because in the dream an angel had girded him as he slept so as to make him, for the future, invulnerable to all temptation to impurity; and this girding by the angel was said to be severely painful.

I believe that this event, or what is meant by it, has something to do with what we have called the relationship to truth. Thomas, as with Goethe, often referred to the knowledge of truth as subject to the condition of purity. Thomas thought of purity as a presupposition for the full realization of the knower's relationship to reality in all its spheres (not just, for example, to the intellectual sphere, but precisely also to this visible world which speaks to all our senses!). Perhaps, in St. Thomas's opinion, precisely the *inner fruit* and the essence of purity lies in the "selfless-ness" and simplicity of this free and natural relationship to reality, not disturbed by the voice of the decadent, plea-sure-seeking self. This shows us why, for example, Thomas sees the beatitude "Blessed are the pure of heart, for they shall see God" as related to the *donum intellectus* (gift of in-tellect). In this context he interprets purity expressly as the inner possibility of awareness of divine reality. It becomes more understandable that Thomas considers blindness of the mind (caecitas mentis) as the first-born daughter of un-chastity: everything opposed to the virtue of prudence de-rives from unchastity; not only the strength to make decisions is undermined by impurity, but the innermost capacity to be open to being is dulled and weakened; the ability of the soul to attend in silence to the language of real things is weakened. But precisely this: being open to the truth of real things and shaping ourselves and the world according to the truth we have grasped—precisely this, according to St. Thomas, is what constitutes the essence of genuine human existence. Not only is it impos-sible, without chastity, for truth to satisfy the mind, accord-ing to Thomas's teaching about temperance, but also: only

a chaste life of the senses is able to realize the human possibility of appreciating physical beauty—for example, of
the human body—as beauty, and to enjoy it for its own
sake (propter convenientiam sensibilium) without the confusion and impurity which arise from the pleasure-seeking
self which clouds everything.

In short: to hear the language of being with complete
naturalness, to grasp the truth of things in reality—precisely this was the real passion of St. Thomas, and one can
regard that event in San Giovanni as a gift of grace, a kind
of existential preparation and anticipation of the attitude
towards reality which has been formulated above in a theoretical and abstract way. It is the attitude of that openness
to the world which radiates without being at all dulled.
Thomas was able, by virtue of this attitude, in his listening
silence, to attend fully to the truth of being—taking it in
so purely that all things tasted to him as they really are
(which, according to an old saying, is the essence of wisdom); and he was so strong in grasping things, so very
capax universi, that nothing in the realm of being is excluded (precisely this is what characterizes St. Thomas's
view of the world: there is nothing that does not belong
to it).

This "complete lack of all pretension," as Goethe formulated it, is also the root reason why Thomas can com-
bine both the insatiable and the unswerving attention to
reality and the relaxed cheerfulness of not being able to
understand. Thomas is not concerned with taking control
of being but of becoming aware of what it is; but being itself—and this is a fundamental conviction of St.
Thomas—being as being is mysterious, i.e., inexhaustible,
incomprehensible for created intelligence. Thus, the fact
that he is aware that he cannot comprehend is also a form

of knowing and acknowledging that which is. Therefore the fact that he ultimately fell silent, that he refused to complete the *Summa theologica,* is not to be attributed to diminishing life forces. Instead, it is a question of a most extreme affirmation of the relation to truth which had been characteristic of him for ages. It is his now heroic selflessness in addressing reality and in listening in silence which is expressed in the words which, so to speak, both end and at the same time complete his existence as a teacher: "All that I have written seems to me like chaff compared with what I have seen and what has been revealed to me."

Corresponding to the passion he brings to fostering this relationship to truth and to the contemplative element he lived with extreme intensity, without which, as we said at the beginning, teaching is not possible in the most real and genuine sense—corresponding to this *first* presupposition of the great teacher is Thomas's no less intensive lived attention to the listeners. Such a link cannot be taken for granted as something obvious. There are great thinkers and researchers who do not have the ability or the will to communicate as teachers. Goethe, for example, although quite akin to Thomas in his attitude of selfless awareness of reality, said of himself that he was more concerned to penetrate the essence of things than to express himself in "speaking, handing on, teaching ...." He once said in a letter to Schiller that he was not given the gift of teaching. — However, as we have said, both elements are deeply characteristic of Thomas: grasping truth in contemplation and actively guiding others to the truth. Leading a person from error to truth is, as Thomas says in his commentary to Dionysius the Areopagite's "On the names of God," the greatest good deed which it is possible to do for another.

The part of Thomas's work written at the request of a friend, a prince, or someone or other unknown to him, constitutes no small part of his complete works. Thomas spent the most energy and the longest period of his life not on writing a work of research (so to speak) but on a textbook—and, indeed, on a textbook for beginners: the *Summa theologica*. "Since a teacher of Catholic truth should not only teach advanced students but also beginners—according to the word of the Apostle "Like little children in Christ I gave you milk to drink, not food" (1 Corinthians 3, 1), therefore we have decided that in this work we would present, in a way that is suitable for beginners, anything related to the Christian religion." He writes this in the prologue to the *Summa theologica*. We will now deal briefly with this prologue.

First we can consider for a moment how truly the teacher is characterized by the fact that he makes an effort—a successful effort—not only to speak and formulate, starting from the initial situation of the beginner, but also to think. This is something that goes far beyond the sphere of the "methodical" and the "didactic" and pedagogical skilfulness; or rather the methodically disciplined skilfulness, which can be learned, is linked here with something much deeper which cannot be learned, with something that can only be described as the fruit of love, of a loving attitude to the listener, even the loving identification with the beginner. In genuine learning more is involved than mere intellectual appropriation: namely, growing into a spiritual reality which the student, from a purely intellectual perspective, is not yet able to grasp but which becomes accessible because of his uncritical trust and belief based on loving identification with the teacher. In the same way, the teacher, insofar as he is able to identify himself lovingly with the beginner through this "love stratagem" (as Nietzsche called it), gains something which is not given to the mature person who, though in many aspects of life—including thinking—is competent, is not free in himself. The teacher will find himself able to become aware of reality like the beginner, with all the un- inhibitedness, with the wonder of a "first encounter" (one might say: like Adam the first time he looked up to see a bird or an apple)—and yet with the practiced and devel- oped ability of the trained mind to penetrate and grasp things. One can say that this fruit of the genuine teacher's love was accorded to St. Thomas in full measure and that it is this which gives the *Summa theologica*, the "textbook for beginners," this unfading youthfulness, the freshness of its statements, the simplicity of diction, and despite all commitment to tradition, fundamental originality. It is surely this charisma which gives to the works of the really great the character of classical simplicity—so that Lao- Tzu, Plato, Thomas are much "easier to read" than the works of their commentators and imitators.

In the case of the *Summa theologica*, of course, there is the added mastery of the didactical trade, and we owe it to this that the gigantic opus never becomes tiresome. The material is divided into 3000 articles, each being, on aver- age, one page in length, and the scholastic *articulus* in it- self, with its formal structure, something much more alive than modern scientific books with their monolog charac- ter. The *articulus* is not a monolog. It is a conversation, a dialogue, a philosophizing with one another (as are Plato's works). I said that "in itself" the scholastic "artic- ulus" is something much more alive than the modern sci- entific form of presentation; we do feel that the *articulus* is not at all alive, but dead, condemned to the dust of the past. Why? Because the conversational form is schematized and because the content of these objections and arguments are, for the most part, alien to us. But if one were to try today to begin a presentation with brief accounts of opposing views, with lively counter arguments which are today considered decisive and crucial, followed by a likewise brief and precise systematic exposition of the subject up for discussion and with, finally, on the basis of this exposition, an answer to the counter arguments—I suspect that this would come across as something incredibly alive.

A brief statement is in order regarding the technical aspects, without which the approach to the truth cannot be managed and about which Thomas speaks with critical awareness, precisely in the prologue to the *Summa theologica*. Seeing things initially from the beginner's angle, he identifies three hindrances which make it difficult or impossible for the novice to grasp the truth and which then threaten to destroy the point of teaching.

Here Thomas speaks first about the revulsion produced by the humdrum and constant repetition of the same thing. For Thomas it is not a question of making a subject "interesting" in some way or other, in order to make it easier for the student. Thomas does not see that things must be made easy for the student at all costs. What concerns Thomas is the following: not just philosophizing, but that all knowledge that penetrates more deeply begins with "wonder"; if that is the case, then it is crucial that the student be led to an awareness of the "wonderful" aspect of the subject to be studied—to become aware of the *mirandum*, the "new." If this succeeds, something more and something different is done than making study entertaining. Namely, the student has indeed made progress, in that he now sees that, in the matter under discussion, how

in all things in created reality the central is far from obvious. It is astonishing, deeper than it appears to ordinary
everyday thinking. (Thus and not otherwise will we have
to understand the report of St. Thomas's contemporaries:
that the students of the Paris university were enthralled
by the newness of his teaching. Thomas was aware of the
teacher's task: to keep the ancient truth present to the listeners in watchful language which is alive and able to express it ever anew.)

According to Thomas in the prologue, another hindrance to teaching and learning to be avoided is the inappropriate division of the material to be learned. What he
means is this: it is not a question of dividing up the material arbitrarily—according to latitude and longitude, so to
speak—with a view to providing an overview and making it manageable; instead, it is a question of showing
clearly the order of things as it becomes clear from the
subject itself; and, while showing the essential inner structure, at the same time revealing the hinges of the structure
by virtue of which one thing is connected with another.
Let us take as an example the three-fold division of the
Summa theologica itself: "Firstly we will treat of God, then
of movement towards God of creatures gifted with spirit,
and thirdly of Christ who—in His humanity—is the way
for us to reach God." This is undoubtedly more than a just
a handy way of dividing up the immense material; in this
division the whole ordered structure of the universe is
made visible; the division itself makes a statement about
the essential reality of the world—and, at the same time,
from a purely formal point of view, a plausible, memo-
rable, and elegant lucidity characterizing the whole is
achieved (whereas none of this can be said of the usual
contemporary divisions of theology into Dogma, Moral

Theology, Liturgy, or even into biblical, historical, systematic, and practical theology).

We have spoken of the "technical" aspect; it is now clear that this expression is perhaps limited too strictly to external things. At least Thomas means by it something that is very intimately linked with the living process of relating to the truth, to reality, to God and the world (or with the thwarting of this process).

This is particularly true of the third hindrance to teaching which is spoken of in the prologue to the *Summa theologica*: the overload of unnecessary erudition and the lack of genuine simplification. Martin Grabmann says that, in the *Summa theologica*, Thomas just dropped, for the first time, "an enormous amount of *inutilia argumenta*," finicky arguments which already become part and parcel of scholasticism in the thirteenth century. But Thomas's ability to simplify things is in evidence not just in this negative way. What happens, then, in genuine simplification? (There are also false, impermissible simplifications; and perhaps one can say that here, in the impermissible, objectively inappropriate simplifications the most dangerous shortcomings of teaching are to be found—demagogy, the distortion of genuine teaching, is based on impermissible simplifications!) The true simplifier (the counter image are the *terribles simplificateurs* anticipated by Burckhardt) does not forget, nor does he let it be forgotten, that the world is extremely many-sided, has many different layers, and is fundamentally incomprehensible and mysterious; but at the same time he knows that this mysteriousness is not contradictory, is not nonsense, not darkness. It is light—of course, light which is so excessive that it cannot be exhausted. It comes from one source of light, from God, the maxime unus, "one" in the ultimate sense, for which reason creation is fundamentally unified and "simple." We

should not overlook in St. Thomas's writings this "othe side" of the so evident clarity (we should not ignore the fac that the first sentence in the teaching about God in the *Summa theologica* is: We do not know what God is, only what he is not—and that at the beginning of the *Summa Contra Gentiles* it is said: here we should have recourse to reason, which all must agree with, but which with regard to divine things is found wanting). Genuine simplification, if it is not to become falsification, presupposes a deeper grasp of reality.

This kind of simplification which is faithful to reality characterizes the superb chapter of the *Summa Contra Gentiles* [4, 11], in which St. Thomas undertakes, in a truly exciting vision of the world, to portray the inner structure of the whole of reality from the stone up to the angel and even into the Trinity. The more a living process is inward, and the more the fruit of this process remains inward (as Thomas says here), the more the living thing itself is of a higher order: thus the fruit of plant life, growing from within, but nourished by forces which are *external*, eventually falls outward (the nut falls from the tree and fruit ripens and falls); and thus also the fruit of sense life, based on what the senses perceive, remains within, although it, too, has its origin from outside; and so the circle of being—in a state of becoming—is completely closed in spiritual / intellectual life; but also the spirit, in the lower, human order of being needs the outside, whereas the angels are purely inward beings in a higher sense, and in God the inwardness of life has that extreme intensity which can only be thought of as the *identity* of essence and life, of tree and fruit, of speaker and word.

This unique simplification is so completely in accordance with reality, it is based on such elementary insights

which cannot be surpassed or overtaken by any refining of research methods applied to nature that a present-day biologist has been able to use this text of St. Thomas as a basis for a modern presentation of the levels of life.

Here I must conclude this series of comments about the intellectual stature of St. Thomas as a teacher. I hope it has become clear that the quality of the "teacher" is not something added but is, instead, a profoundly inner characteristic; so that one can take the words at the beginning of the *Summa Contra Gentiles*—although they are mainly intended to express the aim of that particular work and Thomas is expressing himself here only indirectly, as if quoting—also as a kind of self-characterization: although it is beyond his own forces, in obedience to God he undertakes the work of a wise man, namely, to make known the truth; and then he continues: "To use the words of Hilary: 'I am aware that I owe it to God to see *this* as the special duty of my life, that all my thinking and speaking should tell of Him.'"

"I Feel Absolutely Safe"
Remembering Peter Wust
(1950)

In the legacy of Peter Wust there must be the small note-book in which, during the last weeks of his so disturbingly painful illness, he used to write down his contribution to the conversation—questions, answers, agreement, concerns—at a time when speaking had already become impossible for him but the need to communicate had lost none of its vehemence. The last conversations of the philosopher should be retrievable through the memories of different colleagues with the help of these entries.

The above heading to this short note was entered in that little book, in the still energetic, definite handwriting of this philosopher who wrote impulsively from the depths of the inner person. The sentence is his only contribution to the conversation, which was also the last one we had. The fact that we both sensed this gives his utterance special weight, almost the character of a bequest. I know exactly how, in the unexpectedly full and forceful manner in which Peter Wust spoke, it would have sounded.

I never belonged to Peter Wust's inner circle, but no particularly intimate knowledge was required to know how much the subject of his closely argued and most enduring book "Uncertainty and Daring" (Ungewissheit und Wagnis) was also his most personal theme. This man, of slight build and with fine limbs—almost disembodied—was extremely sensitive and nervous. It was as if his vitality was burned away by the uncontrollable flame of intellectual passion, and he was naturally able to sense the dangers of existence with the sensitivity of a seismograph, so that threats which the average man would hardly notice saw a shattering response which often seemed close to exploding his frame. And nothing was enough completely to disturb him and cause turmoil; sometimes he treated harmless ruggedness as a deliberate, planned slight; the merest problems with his health were handled in the exaggerated manner of the hypochondriac. When people said that Peter Wust could not be persuaded to visit someone who had a cold it was certainly not a legend (which does prove his popularity)—but it did have the quality of a successful caricature.

Of course, all of that is not said for the gratuitous pleasure of keeping alive our memory of things which are only too human, but only on the basis of this phenomenon will it be clear why those words at our last meeting seemed to me to have an element of magic. It may also explain why the aspect of danger, insecurity, risk seemed to be as it were familiar to Peter Wust by his very nature. I remember very clearly a chance meeting with him on the cathedral square in Münster: Wust began out of the blue, almost without any greeting, to speak of the three levels of human insecurity— and this in such a rapt and eccentric fashion and with such unswerving and exclusive focus of his interest that he simply forgot the accepted norms of polite behaviour.

During the long weeks of his last illness I had become a little closer to Peter Wust. Previously we had never met so regularly. In the early spring of 1940—it must have been the beginning of March—I paid him my last visit. My intention was to bring him, as I thought, some consoling news.

At the time, air-raid alarms were still very rare and consequently very disturbing. One morning, and at a time which was also unusual, the sirens were accidentally set off. At my military post where I was working I very soon found out that there no enemy airplane had been observed. I immediately thought of Peter Wust and imagined how unsettled this man must be feeling: he was fearful, helpless, and no longer able to get out of bed. During a short break from work I drove out to him quickly with the somewhat superior attitude of one who has news to pass on which he himself has only just found out about. I found the sick man relaxed in an almost cheerful way, and it was immediately clear to me that he did not particularly need my news. Still, although feeling a little awkward, I told him—in part to justify my hurried visit at an unusual time of day. He responded with a cheerful gesture and there was the suggestion of a smile on his disfigured face. He reached for his notebook and wrote down his answer. Full of embarrassment, admiration, and amazement as I looked suddenly at a new, the real Peter Wust, just as Phaedo at the bedside of the condemned Socrates "in a strange condition experiencing the unusual combination of joy and sadness at the thought that he would soon die"—I read the words: "I feel absolutely safe."

Experiment with Blindness
(1952)

When we consider the way the world is going we could start to wish that truth could again be manifested in a completely unambiguous form, as something simply overpowering, something really compelling.

The following story will show just how questionable such wishes are, how in an uncanny way human freedom and human weakness—and truth itself—are not at all compelling. The story will describe an experiment, an experiment which of course cannot be repeated by everyone. But perhaps it will be clear to everyone that such a repetition has taken place in every age in the same way or in a similar way. It is an experiment with blindness. One of the main characters is a blind man. What becomes clear in the end is that a person can be blind while enjoying good vision. This kind of blindness is the real theme of our story. One of the characters is a relatively young blind man. Everyone knew him, since all he could do was sit in the street begging. But what does "everyone knew him" mean? People saw his movements, knew his voice and his somewhat vacant and rigid expression. But would they have recognized him in a different environment—for instance, at his evening meal in his parents' house where he lived, or as he was being led home by a child? That is doubtful. This circumstance will assume a certain significance in our story.

Let us reveal the most important point in advance: it happened one day that this man was suddenly able to see again—no, not "again," but for the first time (for he had been blind from birth). The beggar had washed himself in stagnant water—and suddenly he was able to see. Perhaps this washing was not the decisive factor. Something else had preceded it. But first another main character must be introduced, one which is not easy to describe. People did speak of a "miracle worker"; some called him the "good man" and some even the "blessed man." But this is not the really important element of our story. The more important part is that he was suspect. Who found him suspect? And of what did they suspect him? This latter question is hard to answer. The authorities suspected him. But why? They were the only ones who knew. They said he had no regard for the laws and customs. But this was clearly not the real reason for the suspicion. Nevertheless, the man's behavior was in some ways out of the ordinary. And suspicion is also not the right word. It was more like disfavor, nearly hatred. The authorities were afraid of the increasing popularity of the miracle man, of his influence with the undiscerning crowd—and rightly so—although the people, not wanting to fall out with the powerful, were becoming cautious about making their naïve admiration for the man too obvious. It was becoming somewhat dangerous to do so. And, after all, they were really not sure what they were to make of him.

And so this man—himself still fairly young, hardly more than thirty—approached the blind man on the roadside. There was a short conversation in which the beggar heard others taking part; then he felt a finger on his eyes which seemed to apply a kind of ointment to them. At the same time he heard a voice saying he was to wash himself in that pond. Then, as the story goes, he received sight.

This is the beginning of the experiment.

> As Jesus went along, he saw a man who had
> been blind from birth. His disciples asked him,
> "Rabbi, who sinned, this man or his parents, for
> him to have been born blind?" "Neither he nor
> his parents sinned," Jesus answered, "he was
> born blind so the works of God might be dis-
> played in him.
> "As long as the day lasts
> I must carry out the work of the one who sent
> me;
> the night will soon be here when no one can
> work.
> As long as I am in the world
> I am the light of the world."
> Having said this, he spat on the ground, made
> a paste with the spittle, put this over the eyes of
> the blind man, and said to him, "Go and wash
> in the Pool of Siloam" (a name which means
> "sent"). So the blind man went off and washed
> himself, and came away able to see.

I said that this event was the beginning of the experiment with blindness. At the story develops it will become
clear in what sense a plain fact can be incontrovertible.

Amongst the first people to see the beggar walking
along the street, even some of his neighbours, there were
those who simply maintained that this was not the same
blind man who had sat in the street for years. Others, of

course, said: it is him, there is no doubt. You just have to look at his face, his hair, the same shabby clothes—everything exactly identical! But the others insisted: no, there are certain similarities, but it is a different person. Well, you could ask the man himself. And his answer was, naturally, to describe what had happened. But what did he know about it? If the "blessed man" had walked by him at this moment he would not have known him. As yet he had not seen him! And so his answer to the ironical question, "who was the person who healed you?" had to be that he did not know. One can imagine the superior attitude of the critical minds on learning that the case was solved beyond doubt. A blind man, one who was supposed to have been previously blind, and an asocial type into the bargain, claims he has been "healed" by that person whom people are always talking about; and then it turns out that it did not even happen in the presence of that miracle worker; the fellow had only heard about him. He does not even know him. No, that is only a badly made-up story.

> His neighbours and people who had earlier seen him begging said, "Isn't this the man who used to sit and beg?" Some said, "Yes, it is the same one." Others said, "No, he only looks like him." The man himself said, "I am the man." So they said to him, "Then how do your eyes come to be open?" "The man called Jesus" he answered "made a paste, daubed my eyes with it and said to me, 'Go and wash at Siloam'; so I went, and when I washed I could see." They asked, "Where is he?" "I don't know" he answered.

The experiment continues further, but first one special circumstance which is indeed a little confusing must be mentioned. The miracle man, as we have mentioned, was not considered to be a respecter of laws and customs. And not only were there many customs, but they were also very strictly observed. For example, there were days on which one would not get one's hands dirty for any money in the world; this would have been considered almost a crime. Now why would that man, precisely on that day, daub the eyes of a blind beggar with a dirty paste made up of spittle and dirt off the street! Anyway, he did. And it is no surprise that the whole thing took on the character of a public provocation. In any case the beggar, stunned by what had happened and defenceless against what others decided, was brought before the authorities. Again he described, very briefly and somewhat impatiently, what had happened to him. Then the authorities divided off into two groups; one of them considered the neglect of the customs to be the crucial element—and as a result the healing was impossible; whereas the other group pointed out that someone who can heal the blind cannot be a bad person. What did the supposedly healed man himself say? He thought he was a great man! Of course, understandably. But he did not even know his "great man." The result was that no one any longer believed the story. It was not true. It could not be true.

> They brought the man who had been blind to the Pharisees. It had been a Sabbath day when Jesus made the paste and opened the man's eyes, so when the Pharisees asked him how he had come to see, he said, "He put a paste on my eyes, and I washed." Then some of the

Pharisees said, "This man cannot be from God: he does not keep the Sabbath." Others said, "How could a sinner produce signs like this?" And there was disagreement among them. So they spoke to the blind man again, "What have you to say about him yourself, now that he has opened your eyes?" "He is a prophet" replied the man. However, the Jews would not believe that the man had been blind and had gained his sight.

Was there no way of finding out whether the beggar, who used to sit on the street before everyone's eyes, was one and the same as this young man whose eyes were clearly sound and who maintained that he had been blind and had suddenly been healed? (Had he perhaps not been really blind?) How could one find out the truth about what had happened? Now, if anyone would know it would be the parents. And so they were sent for and questioned. But it was more like an interrogation. And this is precisely what ruined everything. Of a socially lower class and not able to cope with the carefully phrased questions, became frightened. They had heard that anyone who spoke favorably of the miracle worker was to be ostracized. And this was not something to be taken lightly. And after all, what did they have to do with him? Nothing at all. So they simply refused to give the information. But they did not deny their own son. They admitted that he had been born blind. Surely this could not be interpreted wrongly. But: How is it that he can now see? They knew nothing about that, nothing at all. Besides, the young man was old enough to speak for himself and was not dumb.

They finally called the parents and asked them: This is your son of whom you say he was born blind? How does it come about that he can now see? His parents answered them: we know that this is our son and that he was born blind. But we don't know how he is now able to see. Ask him yourselves. He is of age. Let him do the explaining himself. — The parents said this for fear of the Jews, for the Jews had decided amongst themselves: if anyone acknowledges Jesus as the Christ he is to be expelled from the synagogue. This is why the parents said: He is old enough. Ask him yourselves.

But why was it really necessary to find out what the parents thought about the healing? There was no doubt in their minds that the man who could now see was their son who had been born blind and had been blind until yesterday. And so, what was not clear? Of course, it was "unclear" how such a healing was to be explained. But the fact that it had happened? However, the beggar was again brought in for interrogation.

Now it was no longer a question of hearing and listening but precisely of not hearing, of concealing. In a word, the beggar was to be silenced.

As we know, one can achieve this, or try to achieve it, in a number of ways (this time it was not to be successful). "You cannot," the authorities said to the beggar, "naturally you cannot know our reasons. But we are reliably informed that you are wrong. It would be good for you to keep this in mind. Above all, remember this one thing: it is not just anyone who is now speaking to you. It is us. We who not only have knowledge but also power. Give yourself time to think this through, and when you have understood the situation, tell us for the last time: what actually happened." It is not quite clear whether the beggar was at all aware of the threat contained in these words. He was probably too simple for that. But he suddenly felt so completely fed up with talking that he fell into a rage. It was to his advantage (so to speak) that he was completely lacking in the art of achieving justice. What he had managed to "learn" was how to have passers-by give him alms; and that had been enough. No matter what, the beggar answered the demands of the authorities in an unexpectedly cheeky fashion; he could not resist the mocking question whether they themselves had decided to join the disciples of the blessed one. And instead of acceding to their wish to tell the story again he set about proving to them that not he but they, the powerful ones, were in the wrong. Naturally the result was that they threw him out.

> So the Jews again sent for the man and said to him, "Give glory to God! For our part, we know that this man is a sinner." The man answered, "I don't know if he is a sinner; I only know that I was blind and now I can see." They said to him: "What did he do to you? How did he open your eyes?" He replied, "I have told you once and you would not listen. Why do you want to hear it all again? Do you want to become his disciples too?" At this they hurled abuse at him: "You can be his disciple," they said "we are disciples of Moses: we know that God spoke to Moses, but as for this man, we don't know where he comes from." The man replied, "Now here is an astonishing thing! He has opened my

eyes, and you don't know where he comes from! We know that God doesn't listen to sinners, but God does listen to men who are devout and do his will. Ever since the world began it is unheard of for anyone to open the eyes of a man who was born blind; if this man were not from God, he couldn't do a thing." "Are you trying to teach us," they replied, "and you a sinner through and through, since you were born!" And they drove him away.

The beggar had still not seen the person to whom he owed his sight. But it did not last long until they met one another. The blessed one had not remained ignorant of all the questionings and of the outcome of the last interrogation. And he had deliberately managed it that the beggar suddenly stood before him in the busy market place. He addressed the healed man and asked him bluntly and out of the blue whether he believed in the person who could do superhuman things. Tired of such questions, the man was mildly wondering where the question was leading; and his answer sounded slightly evasive: let him see this person and then the question of belief would be settled. But the beggar had scarcely finished speaking when he hesitated, closed his eyes—like someone who was listening intently—in order to hear the voice of the other in the darkness that was so familiar to him, or rather to recognize it. And then, when the voice then said: this person is standing in front of you, the beggar suddenly understood. Suddenly he realized that precisely in this moment just past he had really begun to see. This joy penetrated him like a flash of lightning and knocked him flat to the ground—while the blessed one, pointing to the man on the ground, said something obscure about the blind who see and those who see and yet are blind. It is fairly certain that no one knew what he meant. And then as one of the bystanders, a member of the powerful group, said in a threatening and mocking tone that this meant that they, the powerful ones, were also blind, the answer came that this is exactly what is wrong: that they are not blind. There was no one now who would have asked what this meant; people wondered if it had any meaning at all.

This was the end of the experiment with blindness.

> Jesus heard that they had driven him away, and when he found him he said to him, "Do you believe in the Son of Man?" "Sir," the man replied "tell me who he is so that I may believe in him." Jesus said, "You are looking at him; he is speaking to you." The man said, "Lord, I believe," and worshipped him. Jesus said:
> "It is for judgment
> that I have come into this world,
> so that those without sight may see
> and those with sight turn blind."
> Hearing this, some Pharisees who were present said to him, "We are not blind, surely?" Jesus replied:
> "Blind? If you were,
> you would not be guilty,
> but since you say, 'We see,'
> your guilt remains."

Did I say that the experiment with blindness is now finished? That would not be exactly true. It would be inaccurate. The account of the experiment is finished, but the experiment itself continues.

Notes 1

The blind spot in the eye is the point where the optic nerve is found. This fact seems to me particularly useful as an analogy for the mind, the human knowing faculties: because created, the mind is not able to achieve a full and complete explanation and grasp of the self. Irreducible and indissoluble, the spirit is firmly fixed in the foundation of its being as if by a blind root and navel—a foundation which is not identical with the spirit. It is not given to the finite spirit to be clear about this root and to subsume it into the self; it is not possible to get behind the root of its own being. There is no retina (not even in the spirit—insofar as we are talking about a finite spirit) which can see everything around it; somewhere there is a blind spot. And that is precisely the point where the organ of sight emerges. Precisely because created being is made possible by something outside itself there has to be a blind spot. (1947)

Vita contemplativa—vita activa: John and Peter. I think it is significant that John is the one who recognizes the Lord; but Peter, who is not the first one to recognize him, jumps into the water to meet him (John 21, 7). And in her visions, Anne Catherine Emmerich says about the race of the two disciples to the grave of the risen Lord (John 20:5f): Peter, the first to enter the grave, did *not* see the angel sitting there, whereas John—who was the first to arrive but made way for Peter to enter before him—did see the angel. Thomas mentions in his *Summa theologica* [I, 20, 4 and 3] the problem (dubitatio): the Lord obviously loved John more than Peter although Peter showed Him the greater love ("Simon, son of Jonas, do you love me more than these?" John 15, 16f]. Augustine understood this in the mystical sense: the active life, symbolized by Peter, is a stronger love of God than the contemplative life symbolized by John. The vita activa feels more strongly the burden of this life and longs passionately to be liberated from it and to come to God. But God loves the contemplative life more since he has made it to transcend life on earth. — Thomas then cites other interpretations and concludes with the sentence: "It would be presumptuous to want to decide this, for it is said: 'Motives are weighed by the Lord (Proverbs 16, 2) and by no one else." (1945)

Immorality begets blindness of the spirit, caecitatem mentis—so say the ancients. Immorality destroys man's pure relationship to the world. And this is not a so to speak separate effect, but this "blindness" is the destructive nature of immorality itself. The disturbance of one's relationship to the world through immorality has three aspects. The first two concern man's relationship to the world as objective being, and the third concerns man's relationship to the world as the totality of being. ("World" always has this double aspect: first, "objective reality" and, second, "the totality of what exists.") The first aspect of this disturbed relationship to the world is: loss of "transparency," of the porousness of being; the second aspect is the shift of focus away from the real and the objective to the subjective; the third aspect is the overpowering of the spiritual ability to decide: the sensual force of desire is fixated on one thing—"ad unum" (a characteristic of unspiritual nature)—whereas the spirit essentially confronts the totality of things in the real world. (1942)

Remorse and fidelity presuppose a good memory; it is the basis of continuity in the life of the spirit. (1927)

"If you do not become as children ..." I have often asked myself: what aspect of the child is meant by that phrase from the New Testament. I think it is the openness—unreservedness—and simplicity with regard to reality and to what is required. Reservation means wanting something "extra" for oneself. The virtue of prudence, in its ultimate and real meaning, includes this lack of reservedness. (So that also from this angle it would appear to be true what I have always maintained, that the "wisdom" of the snake and the "simplicity" of the dove which the Scripture requires of us mean exactly the same thing.) (1942)

If it is the case that anyone who wants to perceive reality must be silent this implies that he is does not merely remain silent to an equally silent world out there but that things "speak." Spinoza says things are mute. In saying this he expressly wants to oppose the concept, handed down in the old theory of being, of the "truth of things." According to this concept, things speak to the perceptive mind about themselves, and anyone who knows how to listen in silence is able to experience no less than the essence of the world, which nevertheless always remains incomprehensible.

But if the world falls silent for the listener (but only one capable of speech can fall silent) then there is, in a special sense, space for God to speak. An old eulogy proclaims: "When God's silence embraced the universe and night was at the summit of its journey, then, Lord, your almighty word sprang down from its regal throne in the heavens." (1943)

Introductory words to a school-leavers' class. — My wish for a young person in this modern age is that he may retain, in the midst of all the optical and acoustic noise of empty stimuli, the noble attitude of silent listening to what is truly real. May he, in the face of the fascinating educational ideal of technically perfect performance, retain the courage to seek true development, which by its very nature remains fragmentary as long as the person himself is "under way." (1952)

Recently I took for the first time—and also for the last time—the well-known stimulant "Pervitin" (methamphetamine), which is often used to excess by young officers. The effect is, in a surprising way, in keeping with the attitude of this age. It produced an almost exaggerated wakefulness and intellectual activity, an enhanced speed in observation and perception. This amounted to a heightening of everything in our knowing process that is engagement and activity of the subject. On the other hand, the "inner calm at sea," which belongs to receptive vision and contemplation, disappears. (1942)

The sentence "Agendo patimur esse" which I thought up and noted down in 1927, taking particular pleasure in the succinct formulation, still holds today. In and through our activity we bear our existence. That includes, first, the fact that being is a gift to us, i.e., that we do not account for it ourselves; second, that it is only given to the active person—and in the measure in which he is active. (1942)

The end of philosophy (the beginning of which is amazement)? — Creation cannot stop keeping something truly amazing in store for us. But what perhaps could happen is that man, devoted to the fabrication of feelings of control over nature, would become incapable of amazed response. (1947)

The horizon of the concept "silence" has astounding dimensions which we experience not only in the wise men's teachings about life. It also has a considerable place in the history of world interpretation. It stretches from the cosmogony of the Hellenistic Gnostics—who saw the unity of the "unnamable" and of "silence" as the world's uncreated foundation in being—to the mystic/ascetic rule of silence of Pythagoras and the monastic orders both of the East and the West, right up to the so charming and profound courtoisie, with which, in Shakespeare's tragedy, Coriolanus greets his wife Virgilia: "My gracious silence, hail!" (1943)

It is one thing deliberately to refrain from speaking words and another thing not to be able to speak because one has been left speechless. Silence of the first kind is human silence in the strict sense, just as the word, containing meaning in sounds made by breath, belongs to the innermost human domain. Where the power of speech fails, man arrives at the limit of his existence. This can be a lower limit or an upper limit. Such a loss of the power of speech may be not so much silence as a becoming mute.

On a journey through Iceland a friend, my hostess, wrote in my travel diary the Nordic saying: Deepest sorrow and extreme joy traverse the earth without words.

There are physical and mental sufferings that, in equal measure, reduce a person to silence by making him powerless and, so to speak, drive him out of his own nature. Rilke, terminally ill, wrote: "Le chien malade est encore chien, toujours. Nous, à partir d'un certain degré de souffrances insensées, sommes-nous encore nous?" (A sick dog is still always a dog. But we, when we pass beyond a certain level of insane suffering, are we still ourselves?) And do not the well-known lines in Goethe mainly invite us to consider that there is a God who freely gave a man—

who had been made mute through his suffering—the gift of speech?

But we lose our speech not only when we are forced down beneath the threshold of our being but also when we are elevated above our ability.

One who, as a mortal being, enters into the light of the divine is blinded, so that just as darkness and the most intense brightness have the same effect on the eye, so also the superabundance of what can be expressed in words becomes inexpressible.

The sphere that is central to human existence, the cultivated field of word and language, borders, left and right, on speechlessness: on the muteness of dumb creatures and on the silence to which the mystic is reduced. But speech drives its roots deep down into the nourishing soil of silence. (1943)

What does living mean? To receive and to embrace is everything. The more reality a being is able to encompass the more it lives. To be alive means to be the beginning and end of one's own journey. (1927)

The fundamental form of willing, which is realized in all individual forms is: loving. Loving means affirming. It is important to see that affirmation and realization are in a certain sense the same. Affirming means wanting something to be (which already is); realization means wanting something to be (that is not yet), effectively wanting something to be. Affirmation is a kind of continuation of realization; and realization is at the same time the most intensive form of affirmation. (1942)

Just as being and not becoming is the real, so too is love superior to wanting to do. (1927)

There are different aspects of activity: doing, the act, the work. There are people who relate to each aspect.

People who *do*, seem to be especially women. They live by doing—without this doing leading to deeds or works. They realize themselves in this plain, humble doing which, so to speak, leaves nothing behind—neither the glory based on deeds nor a lasting work. Perhaps this is what is peculiar to love: to function in a specially selfless way. Male activity takes the form of action and (producing) a work; there are men of action and men who live and function for the sake of a work. A soldier is the prime realization of the man of action; the scholar, the researcher, the artist are the fundamental types who produce works. This diversity in fundamental orientation is revealed in many different ways. The objectivizing which the producer of works aims at is sought by the man of action in the objectivity of social recognition. For the soldier the Iron Cross has a completely different and a much more substantial meaning than the honorary award (Adlerschild) has for the scholar. The real "reward" for the scholar is the work itself, whereas the deeds of the soldier are only fully acknowledged in a manifest acknowledgement by his people. It is in this light that the quite specific "vanity" of the soldier is to be understood. Free time and breaks in activity mean something completely different for the man of action and the producer of a work. The former lives fully and completely only in the time taken up by the act; in the intervening period, in the sometimes long gaps in activity, he is so to speak in the unreal state of "waiting"; he spends the time as one spends waiting time: with playing, distractions, killing time. The other man does not have such periods of waiting; he always has the realization of the work in mind which steadily and constantly grows to fruition. (1942)

A sentence from Dostoevsky's "Demons": A person

who loses contact with the earth also loses his gods." Thomas Aquinas says in terms of knowledge: Error circa creaturas redundat in falsam de Deo scientiam, "an error about creation leads to a false understanding of God." (1942)

Catharsis. — It is strange that purifying activity is ascribed precisely to misfortune. Why cannot joy and happiness purify the person? And what distinguishes the person who is purified by suffering (or also through the experience of tragedy in history) from another person who, under the same circumstances, does not receive such purification? Perhaps it is this: that the person of the first kind exposes himself to the suffering with an attitude of receptive openness to being profoundly moved, whereas the other is closed off and hardened–and thereby perhaps remains more able for life than the former. (1943)

In the "Christian Epimetheus" of Konrad Weiß there is mention of "active contemplation" as a form of consciousness of the metaphysical meaning of history. This innocent kind of awareness is devoid of all aims, even of the highest aims of the human spirit. It is a gift of God. They are not for use. The meaning of history and culture is not to be seen in connection with aims, not from the angle of work but of celebration; not as a concern with justice but mercy. (1946)

Sleep and dream. — In the *Summa theologica* [II, II, 33, 7] Thomas poses the question whether with "fraternal correction" private warning should precede public accusation. In an "objection" that is denied: God also sometimes punishes a person publicly without a previous secret and private warning. Thomas answers this: "Everything hidden is known to God. Therefore the hidden sins are to the divine judgment as the public ones to human judgment; however, God usually corrects the sinner in a kind of private admonition by speaking in him when he is awake or sleeping—as we see in the Book of Job: "In dreams, in nocturnal visions, when deep sleep has fallen on men and they slumber on their beds, He opens their ears and teaches them that he takes people away from the things they are doing." (Job 33,15ff.) (1943)

The need to be conservative comes home to us forcefully again when we see the facile attempts at enlightenment emerging in current discussion of plans for reform. I have reread the *Quaestio de mutatione legum* in the *Summa theologica* in which in an article the question is asked whether human law always needs to be changed as soon as there is something better. Amongst other things the answer says: "When the law is changed, the inner binding force of the law is weakened (vis constructiva legis)." The crucial point is found in the answer to an objection which says: "It seems that the human law has to be changed as soon as something better occurs. For ultimately, human laws, like the other arts, are inventions of human reason ..." Thomas answers this by saying: "Things in art are effective through reason alone, and therefore, as soon as an improvement is possible, a change is to be made. But the laws have, as the philosopher says, their main influence by virtue of custom (ex consuetudine); and for that reason they should not be altered without due reflection." (1947)

From the writings of Thomas Aquinas I have written down some sentences about the *Antichrist.* — In some of these utterances there is special stress laid on the relationship of the Antichrist to Christ. "Just as the head of Christ is God and he in turn is head of the Church so is the Antichrist a member of the devil and yet the head of evil" (III, 8, 8 ad 2). "Just as all good and all virtues of the saints before Christ were prefigurations of Christ so too the tyrants in all the persecutions of the Church are, so to speak, a prefiguration of the Antichrist; the Antichrist was hidden in them; and so all that evil which is hidden in them will be revealed in the time of the Antichrist" (In 2 Thess 2, 1). From this sentence it is clear that Thomas, without hesitation, sees the Antichrist as a political figure. This is borne out in other sentences. The Antichrist, whose arrogance surpasses that of all his predecessors (In 2 Thess 2, 1) "will deceive people firstly through his worldly power, and secondly through his ability to work miracles" (In 2 Thess 2, 2). But here it cannot be a question of a miracle in the strict sense, according to Thomas ("for no one works miracles against the faith, God is not a witness to falseness"); "but sometimes extraordinary things are done which, however, are not beyond the bounds of nature but have hidden causes; precisely such things are done by demons who know the forces of nature and use certain forces to produce particular effects. The Antichrist will also act in this way" (In 2 Thess 2, 2). — The devil, with whose authority the Antichrist will come is already beginning his evil activity in a hidden way: through the despot and seducer; for the persecutions of the Church at this time serve as models for that final persecution against all good people. They are, so to speak, "'imperfect' by comparison with the latter"—as Thomas says in his explanation of the sentence "For the mystery of iniquity doth already work ..." (In 2 Thess 2, 2). In the same context it is also said: "Michael will kill him on the Mount of Olives, the mountain from which Christ ascended into heaven." This is a commentary on the sentence (2 Thess 2, 8) in which it is said that Jesus, the Lord, will kill the Antichrist with the breath of his mouth. And Thomas adds: "In this way Julian was also extinguished by the hand of God" (In 2 Thess 2, 2)—again an indication that the Antichrist is seen in the form of a political ruler. (1943)

"Insofar as we only live for the day and are no longer aware of the extended form of the day or the backdrop formed by darker history—this divine Gethsemane vigil over nature—purely political curiosity emerges. The precursors on the paths of history are half blind, or divided by a trusting blindness, and therefore lacking in a curiosity which will give satisfactory meaning to the day's events." For ourselves and in our political conversations we should keep in mind what is stated in these words of Konrad Weiß. We would see ourselves referred to the obscure and incomprehensible things which are happening in our current history and would see ourselves not merely in a position to handle the daily rush of events with greater, more deeply anchored serenity, but also to judge individual events—which are often enough repugnant to anyone who observes and experiences them at first hand—with greater assurance and justice which would, however, not suggest any element of detachment. (1943)

The "extended form of day," in contrast to the short form with which political curiosity is concerned, reminds us of the thousand years which to God are like one day. This extended form of day contains also what is counter to day—the night—of darker history. It is the night in which what is contrary to all that seems rationally comprehensible takes place as its counterpart. If we see history in relation to sacred history perhaps we can say: just as the night side of Christ's suffering and death is related to the day side of the incarnation of the logos, and this night side of suffering and death is opposed to the "natural" course of things as the "natural" man understands and wants it, so is the night of history beyond the reach of any idealistic attempt at comprehending and interpreting it. And just as in the death and suffering of Christ the genuine incarnation took place—running counter to nature— so too in history as such the completion of its "day" events takes place under the veil of night and is likewise "running counter to nature." This latter can mean many things: it can mean that salvation (which for Konrad Weiß is the entirely elusive meaning of history) is to be had where all appears to be doom and decline—hope against hope. It can also mean that history, as belonging to man, and also man himself, cannot find perfection in the naively wilful in nature but rather that the great upswings of history thwart all that is purely natural and thereby thwarts all predictions. (1943)

The aspect under which C. S. views the political world is so exclusively concerned with the impoverished and perverse forms of everyday reality that a quite cynical denial of "true" reality results. For example, the rejection of the concept *bonum commune*. "Anyone who says *bonum commune* intends to deceive." No matter how much this may apply to everyday political reality, it remains true that there is such a thing as *bonum commune* and that, despite all kinds of abuse, it is achieved. Or he speaks of Pareto and his witty realism; Pareto would, for example, define the elite as follows: those who, while earning the highest income, pay no taxes. In a variation on this theme C. S. says: "the elite today are those who still drive a car." To a certain extent this disillusionist view of the world is justified. But it does not go very far. Instead one could say: there is no human ideal which, when faced with the real world, could not become a caricature and usually does. It seems much more meaningful to ask about the character-istics of a *true* elite and to see that in every age the "best people in a nation" really exist and that they, no matter how narrow their influence as formal leaders, in some way or other perform their leadership function in obscu-rity and are paying the price—even as witnesses in their own blood.

To my mind this shows that, if knowledge which is worthy of man and reality is to flourish, our attention must focus on the "truly real" and not on the "bad real-ity": the shallow foreground noise of "life" that masquer-ades as the true form of reality. (1942)

There is a melodramatic way of speaking which plays a role in the Exercises and in popular Missions: life and all things must be seen "in the light of the funeral candle," since only then do we see them for what they are: namely, as of no value—but at least real and important insofar as in them God has presented us with a task. Precisely this is what I think is behind some characteristic statements in existentialism: things are seen "in the light of the funeral candle"—except without what is still a positive element in the Christian conception of death (leaving aside, of course, the romantic petit bourgeois idyll that is expressed in the "funeral candle"). The world, things, life become a matter of complete indifference—but not by comparison with the supremely positive, the transcendent world, eternal life. They become completely nothing because they lack the counterbalance of the transcendent. Sartre's story "The Wall" describes the last hours of people con-demned to death: how the complete meaninglessness of everything gradually becomes clear, so much so that the question of "release or not" is a matter of indifference. "To wait a couple of hours or a couple of years is all the same when one has lost the illusion of immortality." Once this "illusion" has gone everything that is mortal is completely devoid of meaning. But we should not confuse the despair which arises from this with the "contempt for the world" which is possible on the basis of a life in God's love—the highest affirmation of the highest reality. (1947)

Traditionalism. — In times of upheaval and great historical change people who are searching for the right reaction to and fitting evaluation of things realize how little help is to be found in reason alone, even when it is "enlightened by faith." It is not a matter of a theoretical weighing up of propositions but of saying yes or no to streams of historical development which, swollen from different sources, wash around us, sometimes all the more vigorously for having been dammed up. We then learn how much security is to be found in tradition—tradition understood both in the most common everyday sense and in the ultimate and finest sense in which the Church understands it and as it is found in relation to the most ancient revelations. But if it is also true that, as is always the case in times of great historical change, the rationalists try, for their part, to channel the stream into a bed and to make of human society an ordered wilderness, the temptation to see in tradition the exclusive principle of historical legitimation has become very big and almost inevitable. Thus it was a kind of cultural necessity that the French Revolution resulted in traditionalism, and probably the epoch of "total planning" will give birth to the opponent of a new traditionalism. A clear sign of this is to be seen in the turning towards a "primitive age" which is understood as an archetype and model. (1942)

If the myths of various peoples may and must be understood as "remnants of primeval revelation," Christians and theology should have more reverence for the myths and the teachings handed down from the past by one's own people and also for those of the "heathens." The value of primitive revelation, it seems, is one of the most currently relevant teachings of Christianity in the age of the "one world." (1942)

The way a person feels about life seems to be determined partly by the level of his success in carrying out the task assigned to him by his calling or profession, but even more by his insight into the impossibility of the task being properly fulfilled—but also by the conviction that it could be fulfilled. The house that the builder has constructed is finished. The lawyer's case is "won," brought to a conclusion by a final legally justified judgment. By contrast, the task of philosophical reflection—and also of theological meditation—can, of its essence, not be completed. But then there is the happiness and "remaining young" that come with it.

The intrinsic division of all earthly power between Emperor and Pope ("that the marrow is split and knowledge is not the same as life," as Konrad Weiß says in *The Christian Epimetheus*), so that neither can be replaced by the other and neither can do without the other—this split is, so to speak, the emaciated and deficient form of the concept *bonum commune*. Abstractly it can be said that the point of political power is to achieve the *bonum commune*. But historically this concept immediately suffers the fate of being split in two. (1943)

Christians and their sacred book. — "Imagine if an educated Indian, who has grown up in the world of the Hindu books of wisdom and is now trying to understand the basic ideas of Christianity, were to ask you about the following: what does it mean that a God gives to a redeemed person a white stone on which a name is written that no one knows except the person who receives the stone. What would your answer be?" — Recently I posed this question to a group of about fifty Catholic students. Silence, surprise, slight amusement at such a strange question. Not one of them saw that the question referred to a sentence from the New Testament, no less! (1953)

On the relationship between the angels and men Thomas has an interesting text (*Summa Contra Gentiles* 3, 91): "Human concerns are connected to higher causes and are not simply adrift. For the decisions and desires are directly determined by God; human knowledge, which belongs to the sphere of reason is directed by God, with the angels as intermediaries; but all that belongs to the physical realm and, whether internally or externally, comes to be used by men, is directed by God with the angels and the heavenly bodies as intermediaries." Then this three-fold thought is developed in three short paragraphs; in the second paragraph, human knowledge—manifold, changing, capable of error—is compared with that of the angels which is characterized as unified, unchanging and incapable of error. And then follows the interesting sentence: "It is therefore necessary that our intellectual knowledge be guided by the knowledge of the angels." (1942)

If one reduces the statements of psychiatry to a common denominator insofar as they try to achieve a more general definition of neurosis beyond giving mere symptoms, the result is as follows: neurosis is the result of a wrong response to objective reality, above all to society; it is the attitude of a misfit, it is loss of connection with reality, preoccupation with self; aversion to sacrifice; more devoted to appearance than capable of being; it is a case of a meaningless, nonsensical life; it will be healed when the sick person finds the meaning of life again; neurosis is remote in the measure that a person is grounded in the sphere of the "higher values of existence." — All of these things are fundamental categories which concern human life as a whole, the most purely ethical categories. The question is: under what conditions does the ethical failure—which is clearly much more frequent than neurosis—become the cause of such sickness?

"Manic depressive." — The world is so set up that anyone who were to have clear insight into it could fall into an abyss of sorrow: God's own *logos*, having become man, had to die an awful and shameful death; at the end of world history there is to be world domination by evil; Thomas Aquinas says that the beatitude "blessed are those who mourn ... " is appropriate to the experience of scientific knowledge. Pondering this (and we can do this without conscious reflection) we could burst into tears and experience the deepest depression—which does not have to be unrelated to reality and have no foundation. And on the other hand: reality is at the same time, and in no less real a way, interwoven with salvation; it is to such an extent—and in a way which goes beyond all comprehension—carried by God's love that anyone who thinks this through very carefully could be overcome by a joy which also might seem to be without any obvious foundation and which might simply be beyond our grasp. Why is the middle position seen as "normal"? And what regulates this normality? Is it the physiological condition of the internal secretory system or the nervous system? (1947)

II

But now bring me hither a minstrel. And when the minstrel played, the hand of the Lord came upon him …

2 Kings 3, 15

Work – Free Time – Leisure (1953)

It is not immediately obvious from the three terms that they involve an absolutely explosive complex of problems which are not at all purely theoretical. Instead, they give the impression of being almost harmless. Whether we see in the words something positive or something which arouses distrust, they could be seen as an encouragement to take things too lightly. The title seems to radiate a cheerful, even idyllic freedom from problems, increasing from one word to the next: "Work"—that expresses the seriousness of life but with "Free time" that is on the way to being relaxed and forgotten. And finally "Leisure"—one sees the angler who, completely contented with his lot, sits on the edge of a lake in summer, far less interested in what he catches than in just sitting there and dreaming. Where is the problem?

The word and the concept "work" are completely familiar to us. Work is what takes up a person's normal day, it is the satisfying of our needs, the procuring of bread, the active preoccupation with what we require for living. That is all quite clear.

Why is the concept "free time" not equally clear? It is a concept with many strata. As long as I see the concept purely negatively as the length of time which is not taken up with work there is no problem. And even when I see

}143{

free time exclusively in relation to the working day—only as a break from work—here, too, there is nothing particularly problematic. We only become unsettled when we see that we are not at all able to see the time in which we are free of work purely in this light. Previously I used the term "normal day" only in passing and without any agenda. But this notion immediately conjures up another, closely related idea which gives the idea of free time a quite new and positive meaning—a meaning which says that we are no longer dealing with the pure fact of an interruption of work and period of recovery. This other notion is that of the holiday. On the one hand we are not able to suppress this notion of holiday—not yet (here we see the influence of Western tradition); on the other hand, the notion of a holiday has lost definition and depth of meaning. It is no longer taken for granted (which shows how the Western approach to life is being weakened and is under threat). If we ask what a holiday, a feast day, actually means and how a person's live inner festive feeling comes about, how it can be awakened and retained—without which the celebration of a feast cannot be conceived as a concrete possibility—it is to be feared that such questions can no longer be answered by people of our time on the basis of direct knowledge. However, we still have a sense that the seventh day is different from and more than the "weekend"; and we have not yet forgotten the fact that and the reason why the word "holidays" (Ferien) literally refers to a space of time for celebrating. All of this means that the concept free time is not as superficially harmless as it may at first seem. It reaches down into a deeper dimension in which, without clear delimitation, it makes the transition to the third concept, that of "leisure."

We can confidently affirm that we do not know what is meant by it; or, more exactly, we do not know what the concept leisure means in the Western philosophical tradition as formulated by Plato, Aristotle and the great thinkers of Christendom. Well, we could say, why should we know? What does it matter if we do not know? Our notion of man and therefore of the meaning of human existence has, after all, changed since antiquity and since the Middle Ages! This objection is not at all to be taken lightly. Even when one agrees with it—and precisely then—one must see what exactly is up for discussion here. One must realize that the complete and definite decline of the fundamental Western concept "leisure" will have as its quite clear historical consequence: the totalitarian worker state. And if we do not like this consequence we have to see that there can be no resistance to the total world of work, i.e., from an ultimately human point of view—and that means, in the long run, the only adequate resistance—if we do not rediscover and realize the idea: we work in order to have leisure.

But what does this mean? A complex web of ambiguities has to be removed for the true meaning of the statement to become clear. It is essential to spell this out a little. The trouble for us Germans is the awkwardly close relationship between leisure and idleness, a relationship between the words (Muße and Müßiggang); in reality, doing nothing is just the opposite of leisurely activity (the Greeks said: scholén agein). We work in order to have leisure—that would first and foremost mean: we work in order to do something, in order to be able to do something that is not work. What sort of activity is being referred to here? Recreation, entertainment, amusement, play—none of these is meant here. Surely it would be nonsense to think that work is there for the sake of play. What is meant is activity which is meaningful in itself. And work—is it not also likewise meaningful? Meaningful, yes! But not meaningful in itself. That is what the concept "work" consists in: that it serves for something else, that it produces things with a useful value, that it is a contribution of general usefulness (and usefulness always means: being good for something else). Serving some other purpose is essential to the notion of work. This is where the invidious expression "servile work" belongs. It has nothing to do with any kind of belittling of work or of the working person. We can say that the opposite is true. Of course, according to the ancients, there are human activities which serve no practical purpose. There are activities which are not servile. And these are forms of work for every person, also the working person. They are essential, indispensable (just as servile forms of work necessary to meet our needs have to be carried out by everyone).

At this point a word must be said about the distinction between "servile arts" and "liberal arts"—*artes serviles* and *artes liberales*. It is an old distinction which at first seems very old-fashioned, as something of purely historical interest. But it is in fact far from old-fashioned. It even has particular political relevance. Translated into the jargon of the all-embracing world of work it means the following: there is not only production and the fulfilling of the prescribed plan; there are also, and rightly so, human forms of activity which by their very nature cannot be subject to the yard-stick of a five-year plan. Which means that there is human activity which, on principle, does not need justification as part of a social utility plan. When we formulate it in this way it becomes clear what kind of radical heresy, affecting the foundations of the all-embracing world of work, is contained in the old Western proposition: there are free arts—human activities which are meaningful although they are neither work nor recovery from work for the sake of work. And hopefully this also shows how there is a hidden danger, with significant consequences, if we try to deny that work has the character of serving another purpose—the character of "servility." Such a fiction, namely, that work as the production of something useful is meaningful in itself, brings about the opposite of what seems to happen. What happens is exactly the opposite of a "liberation," an "ennobling," a "rehabilitation" of the working person. What happens amounts precisely to the dehumanization of the world of work. It produces the ultimate chaining of the person to the work process—expressly the proletarianization of everybody.

But what in the totalitarian worker state happens expressly is present everywhere in the world as a danger and a temptation. This is seen, for example, in the difficulty of answering the question: what would you identify as an activity which has meaning in itself, a so-called "free" activity? How would you conceive of an activity which did not require legitimation from elsewhere, not as the production of something practical and useful; an activity which does not supply food but which is itself a living value in which the good that is appropriate to the human person—the real human richness, the full possession of life, the utmost satisfaction—is realized?

Clearly, it is only possible to give an answer to this if one has a particular conception of the human person. What concerns us here is nothing less than the fulfilment of human existence. In what does this fulfilment consist? It is not necessary, it seems to me, to look for originality in this. I shall try and formulate what can be learned from the Western philosophical tradition. The most important element is this: ultimate fulfilment, meaningful activity as such, the perfect form of life, utmost satisfaction and a share in the fullness of life has to take the form of seeing—the contemplative awareness of the foundation of the world. The ultimate wisdom of Plato, for example, is expressed in these words: "Here, if anywhere—so said the stranger from Mantinea [Diotima]—here a person feels life is worth living, where he contemplates the divinely beautiful: this makes him immortal."

It takes only one step and we are back in the concrete. Perhaps you have thought, some disconcerted or even shocked, that here some airy-fairy philosophical ideas are being presented. We are back with our very real question: here and now, what constitutes an activity which is meaningful in itself? As I have said, if we are not in a position to answer this question there is no significant possibility of showing resistance to the all-embracing world of work. The answer offered by Western tradition would be this: wherever, when seeing, watching, contemplating—even if from a distance—we make contact with the center of the world, with the hidden, ultimate meaning of life as a whole, with the divine root of things, with the quintessence of all archetypes (and seeing—profound contemplation—is the most intense form of appropriation there is), wherever and whenever we turn in this way to reality as a whole, we are involved in activity which is meaningful in itself.

Such intense attention directed to the roots and foundations of the world, to the archetypes of things—this activity which is meaningful in itself—takes a thousand concrete forms. An especially worthy form which is largely forgotten is religious contemplation, the meditative immersion of oneself in the divine mysteries. Another is philosophical meditation, which is not at all to be seen as limited to a specific academic discipline. Everyone who, while reflecting on human acts and lives is confronted with the unfathomable nature of fate and history or who with quiet attention gazes on a rose or a human face, is confronted with the mystery of creation—all of these are sharing in that which has preoccupied the great philosophers from time immemorial. Yet another form of that activity is the artist's work which is not geared to producing copies of things but to making fundamental images of things perceptible to him and to rendering them visible and palpable in language, sound, color, and stone. But anyone who as a listener grasps the poetic in a poem, anyone who contemplates a work of art the way the artist means it to be seen gains, all things being equal, contemplative contact to the center of the world, to the sphere of the eternal archetypes. "All things being equal"—here is the difficulty. It is precisely the already identified difficulty of seeing all these forms of approaching the world contemplatively as having a meaning in their own right— the difficulty of simply experiencing them and realizing them. Is this difficulty not the underlying reason for the increasing isolation of the artist, the creative writer—but also of the philosophizer and the person dedicated to religious contemplation?

Here we need to speak of some conditions and presuppositions which are to be fulfilled for the realization of this activity which has meaning in itself. At this point they can be named.

First, it is not possible to carry out an activity which is meaningful in itself unless one has an attitude of receptive openness and listening silence—an attitude, therefore, which is completely contrary to the attitude of labor, i.e., of strained activity. It is a fundamental human experience that the great and fulfilling things in life, while perhaps not free of our own strenuous efforts, do not come about through these efforts but come to us only when we able to receive them as a gift.

But here we find a second, deeper presupposition which is still less in our grasp and without which the simple performance of an activity which is meaningful in itself cannot be expected, or rather: without which it cannot be expected that contemplative contact with fundamental reality can be seen as meaningful in itself—whether it be in the form of literature, music, the plastic arts, philosophical reflection, or religious contemplation. This second presupposition is, to put it briefly, that a person must be capable of celebrating a feast day. But what does that amount to? Obviously it is more than a day off from work. It requires that, despite all that is wrong with the world and even through tear-filled eyes, one is able to affirm the ultimate meaning of the world and knows that one is in tune with it and is embraced by it. Living out this affirmation, this harmony, this awareness of being embraced, in a way which differs from the everyday, precisely this is what people have known as a feast day from time immemorial. Here it becomes clear that there is no feast day without gods, that a cultic celebration is the original form of festival. But that is a new theme. — Yet this much has to be said: free breathing room in the middle of one's daily working life can only be had if, on the basis of such an affirmation, forgetting one's needs, one is to be able to do things that are meaningful in themselves. Thus, from another angle, all forms of this "free" activity—above all, the artistic forms—have by their very nature a festive character as long as at least some sense of this affirmation is alive in them. Of course, if it is completely absent, all handling of "free time" must become a different, more breathless and even despairing form of work. It is hardly necessary to demonstrate that this is not an illusory notion, and it is, I think, not completely alien to our experience: that precisely artistic activity could degenerate into an idle game without substance or to a new, more subtle form of frenzied activity, wheeling and dealing and restlessness—if it is not reduced simply to pure entertainment which misleads the person into locking himself up in the world of work and finding himself comfortable in it.

Nevertheless, wherever the arts are based in the festive contemplation of the totality of the world and its foundations, a kind of liberation comes about, a stepping out under the clear skies—both for the artist and for the most modest of beholders of his work. This liberation, this premonition of the ultimate and extreme satisfaction is almost more necessary for man than bread itself, which is both indispensable and at the same time inadequate.

Precisely this, I think, is the meaning of the old Aristotelian proposition from the Nicomachean Ethics: "We work in order to have leisure."

How Do We Learn to See Again? (1952)

1

Man's ability to see is declining—we experience this again and again if we are engaged in education. Of course, this is not a reference to the physiological sensitivity of the eye. What is meant is the inner possibility of grasping visually reality for what it is.

Of course, man has never really seen everything that is visible before his eyes. The world, even in the face it shows us, is unfathomable. Who could exhaust all there is to see of one single wave at sea as it develops and subsides? — But there are degrees in our powers of comprehension, and clearly there is a definite line of demarcation which cannot be crossed without man, even as a spiritual entity, being endangered. It seems that today this point has been reached.

I am writing this as I return from Canada on board a ship sailing from New York to Rotterdam. Most of the passengers have spent a fairly long time in the US, many of them solely with a view to seeing the New World as its guests—seeing it with their own eyes. But this is precisely the problem.

In some of the conversations on deck and at table I am continually surprised to hear, almost exclusively, very summary judgments which are also to be found in the guidebooks. It turns out that hardly anyone has noticed in the streets of New York the numerous little signs pointing to public air-raid shelters. And who would have noticed, in visiting the University of New York, the stone chess tables which a provident local council has built on Washington Square for the benefit of the Italian lovers of the game living in this quarter?

Or: I had, at table, spoken about the glory of the luminous sea creatures which were stirred up in their hundreds in the wake of our ship; the next day someone said in passing that there was nothing to be seen the previous night: they had not had the patience to adjust their eyes to the darkness.

So again: the ability to see is declining.

2

If we ask why, various answers can be given: for instance, the sufficiently criticized restlessness and harassment felt by our contemporaries; or the fact that they are too taken up with and ruled by the need to achieve practical goals. But it must not be forgotten that the average person of our time has lost the ability to see—by seeing too much!

There is such a thing as optic noise, which no less than acoustic noise makes hearing impossible. One might think that people who read magazines and visit cinemas are schooling their eye to see more sharply. But the opposite is true. The ancients knew what they were saying when they called visual delight destructive. And the healing of the inner eye can hardly be expected today—unless one manages to make a firm resolve to exclude from the sphere of one's own life the illusory world of stimuli continually produced by the entertainment industry.

3

One may perhaps object that, admittedly, the capability of seeing is in decline; but such losses are simply the price of all higher culture. Undoubtedly we have lost the keenness of sense enjoyed by the Indians, but we no longer need it now that we have telescopes, compasses, and radar. I have already said that in this no doubt progressive development there is a line, the crossing of which spells danger for man— a danger which directly threatens the integrity of his own being and which cannot be averted by technical means.

The ability to see the world "with one's own eyes" is intrinsic to the innermost constitution of the human being; here his real human richness is at stake, and also, where there is a threat, his most profound impoverishment. Why? Because through vision the original and fundamental conquering of reality begins, and in this the life of the spirit essentially consists.

I am quite aware that there is a reality to which man has access only through "hearing." Yet it is still true that only seeing—seeing oneself—is the foundation of man's independence. If a person can no longer see with his own eyes he can also no longer hear in the right way. It is the person who is impoverished in this way who inevitably succumbs to the demagogic allure of whoever is in power—inevitably, because such a person no longer has the possibility of critical reserve (which indicates the contemporary political relevance of our theme!).

4

Diagnoses are necessary, but they are not enough. So, what can be done?

We have already dealt with the pure abstinence, the simple fasting which will keep at bay the optical noise of daily trivialities. This seems to me to be an essential step but only as the removal of an impediment.

A much more direct and effective remedy is: that we are to produce visual forms by our own hand.

No one's eye must have seen so much of the visible human face as the eye of one who undertakes to reproduce it in a visual image. But this does not apply only to producing an image by hand. The image produced by language succeeds only on the basis of a higher power of vision; what intensity of vision was required for it to be possible to say: "The girl's eyes shone like wet currants" (Tolstoy).

Because giving artistic shape to things is based on seeing, the mere attempt at it demands a new approach to the visible world; it requires a way of seeing things that is one's own. And a long time before the successful production of the work the artist will have gained another inner advantage: more profound openness of his eyes, more intense penetration, higher precision in his grasp of things, more patient receptivity for what is unlikely, perception of what up to this point did not even seem to be there. In a word: he will not only become aware of the richness of the world in a quite new way, but—as if answering a challenge—his own personal ability to take in this enormous harvest will grow. It is his ability to see that grows.

5

It has sometimes been said: the amateur playing of music in families and in youth groups, which is becoming more and more popular and is continually growing, has no counterpart in the sphere of the plastic arts. This explains why modern music has a much stronger and broader popular resonance than modern painting and sculpture. Here we see that it is this active amateur sector which supports the artistic life of a city and therefore also the life of the genuine artist. And if now some efforts are being made in "studios," in schools for artistic production, to train also in this sphere a stratum of active amateurs we must realize that this is not about artistic life seen in isolation. It is concerned with saving people from becoming mere consumers of collective products and obedient followers of managerial directives. The question is how people can retain, undiminished, the foundation of their spiritual life and their direct relationship to reality: the ability, namely, to see with one's own eyes.

Renewed Encounter with a Poem (1942)

On one of the last days of my leave I was busying myself with the drawers of my writing desk in which I had placed, in a not particularly orderly fashion, different kinds of papers—letters, excerpts, half-finished essays, and other writings. My friends, who because of my orderly exterior made assumptions about other aspects of my life, were again and again surprised (and this mostly with undisguised, almost joyful satisfaction) when they caught a glimpse of this hidden lack of order.

It was not my love of rummaging around, or at least not just that, which on this afternoon of thunderstorms and rain caused me to take out my notes again. No, I was also of a mind to protect some of them—especially drafts and plans of future essays—from the destruction which we had to be prepared for in our area.

While pensively preoccupied with this task, for which I would prefer to be shut away in isolation, I came across a blue work book, on the white label of which my name was written in the movingly bold handwriting of a school-boy. At the time it was important for me not to omit my second Christian name, which I changed into a slightly more impressive form. This blue work book contains poems. Not my own, but poems which I had written down from periodicals, borrowed books, the newspapers, because I found them particularly good. For many of the poems there was no indication of their origin. Names of poets meant nothing to me in those years. I was interested in the poems, not the authors. What is worse: in writing them down I was not worried about changing a verse if I thought the rhyme or rhythm did not work. And so it would not be easy from this work book to identify the author and share the information properly with others.

The smile which accompanies our thoughts about former enthusiasms is usually complacent. We believe only too readily how far we have come. And so as I paged through the poems I was not expecting to find anything special. Then unexpectedly my eye and my ear were suddenly engaged and, pausing, I had to read again with careful attention a little poem of two stanzas:

Delicate birch tree, bow down
Deep into the sky,
The evening star enters
Your hanging branches
In its tender surrounds
It shines doubly clear,
A fish in the heavenly weir,
Golden and wonderful.

For how many months had the world looked so different. And so I was in a frame of mind in which even a little poem could give me some satisfaction, but it was only a sort of starved feeling that seemed to be addressed in a particular way. In any case, at this moment I experienced what Goethe, when the world of music opened up and profoundly moved him as a seventy-year-old, expressed in the beautiful image of the clenched fist which one suddenly opens to reveal the friendly palm of the hand.

Happy about finding this treasure, I immediately wrote down the two verses for a second time. Who the poet is who produced them in an inspired moment I do not know. There is no name in the blue work book.

A few days later, on the last day of the holidays, two friends visited me with their wives. One of the friends was convalescing in our town after being severely wounded. We were sitting in the now gloriously fresh garden. In the bright sky swept clear of clouds, we could see, just beginning to emerge, the crescent of the new moon which in these parts has become associated with quite unromantic notions.

It was not long before I told my friends about my discovery.

It should be said that sharing our taste for literature was what nourished our friendship since student days, and so it happened that on this evening, as on many previous evenings, we very soon became engaged in a most lively discussion: by no means inclined to be satisfied with the vague acceptance of an unspoken feeling, we tried to define what formed the "beauty" of this poem which, to my delight, had also struck the others.

The young wife of my wounded friend, not yet fully part of our circle, was quiet from the beginning and remained so. But I thought I saw in her eyes a more than normal interest in our conversation. There was something in her silence that stirred us to the extent that, without realizing it, nearly all of us addressed our thoughts to her. At one point she picked up the little book that lay open on the table and read the two stanzas with close attention as if listening inwardly, and then, again without a word, put the book back.

The conversation began with what was most immediate and demonstrable in the poem: the transparent musicality in the sound of the vowels. The first stanza had the brightness of violins and in the second the celli and the double basses arrived, and as is fitting for a pastoral, then came the woodwind. In the first were the delicately breathed unearthly sounds, in the second there was, by contrast, only fullness, peace and strength. This combination and contrast worked particularly well. In special support of all this was the measured rhythmic progression of the verses, such that the contrast of the thoughts began all over again. The tension of some contrastingly built feet give the first stanza an imperceptibly hesitant and faltering movement, whereas the second in its completely unswerving course empties powerfully in a steep gradient into its conclusion.

What seemed most important to me was to point out the simple clarity of the image which our poem painted with clear and precise silverpoint contours in the evening sky. For was this not precisely what constituted the beauty and purity of the imagery—without any additional element of feeling or description? And I suggested that, with no detriment at all to what had been said so far, herein lay the reason why the poem affected us all so profoundly and in such a special way.

Although my contribution to the conversation was by no means the smallest I was aware on this evening of the inadequacy of our efforts, and it is probable that through her silence our friend was the responsible party. Even if our comments, which were directed more to the formal and technical aspects, were accurate in their detail, I was painfully aware that we had not found the right word to define what was special about this poem. Thus I thought it advisable to divert the course of the conversation, not too obviously, to another subject.

At this point the dark and very quiet voice of our friend, so silent up to this point, made itself heard. Might she add to my conclusion (and here she smiled at me) a second one? The clear lines of the imagery I had referred to had a further special character. The poem referred to the sky not as high, but deep. And the birch tree leaned inwards as well as downwards. What was introduced in this way in the first two verses was completed, in the description of the evening star as the fish in the weir, to become the image of the world sunk both into the night and into the sea. That is why, despite all the crystal clear contours, there are fluid undercurrents and the nocturnal element associated with water. And so the poem itself appears as if written on the fleeting mirror of a surface of water, the clarity of which is threatened at any minute by a breath of wind or by an insect alighting on it. The mystery of the verses and their effect—which will never be completely accounted for—includes this aspect as well.

Then, without needing the work book, she recited the little poem in a slightly louder voice. For a second time the poem, now as if transformed, addressed our inner gaze and ear.

Soon we parted company. The stillness of this night was not disturbed by the war, although the sky was clear from evening till morning. I lay asleep without dreaming, as if in a deep well. When I awoke my leave was over.

On Music
A Speech during a Bach Concert
(1951)

That the philosopher, especially when he is also preoccupied with matters concerning human development, pays special attention to the essence of music, is not to be explained purely by his random personal interests in music. Indeed, this special attention has a great and long tradition reaching back almost to the beginning of history—to Pythagoras and Plato, and also to the teachers of wisdom in the Far East. — It is not just that amongst the "astonishing things" (with which, according to Aristotle and Thomas Aquinas, the philosopher formally busies himself)—it is not just that amongst the *miranda* of the world music is one of the most remarkable and most mysterious things. It is also not just the fact that someone has been able to say that making music is itself simply a hidden form of philosophizing, an *exercitium metaphysicae occultum* of the soul, which of course does not realize that it is philosophizing. (This was Schopenhauer in his profound utterances about the metaphysics of music.) But that which brings music again and again to the attention of the philosopher is its quite special inner significance for human existence; and this is precisely what makes it necessary for everyone involved in education to be concerned with music and music making.

The question which fascinates anyone philosophizing about the nature of music is: what do we really hear when we listen to music? It is undoubtedly something more than and different from the particular sounds produced by the bow on the strings of the violin, or by the air blown into the flute, or by striking keys—even a completely unreceptive person (if there is such a person) hears all of these things. But he does not hear what music really is. Then what is it that we hear when we listen to music receptively? — The question is easier to answer in regard to the other arts—although the question "What do we really see when we contemplate Dürer's The Great Piece of Turf?" is also not easy to answer. It is not grass as we see it—more clearly—in nature or in a photo. It is not the grass, not this "object" which we really see when we contemplate a painting in the right way. Or: what do we really become aware of when we hear a poem, when we become aware of the poetic quality of a poem? Undoubtedly, something more and something different from what is directly said in the poem (which has even been referred to as the impure element of the poem—of course, a necessary impure element). And so these questions are equally difficult to answer. But now the question: what does one hear when one listens to music in a musical way? It cannot be a "subject" like ones in the visual arts or in poetry—where something is presented, something is stated as a subject. In music there can be no question of this, even though this is again and again thought to be the case, even by great musicians. What one really hears when one listens to Beethoven's Sixth Symphony is not the "Scene by the Stream" or the "Storm" or the happy gathering of peasants. But how is it in the case of "song"? Is it not, at least here, the case that we really hear what the text says when an aria or a recitative is sung? Naturally we hear the words. But, in addition to the words, in genuine, great music—when we listen in the right way—we hear at the same time a deeply secret meaning to these words which we don't hear if we listen to the words alone. This deepest meaning is not there to be read like something straightforwardly stated! — *And so, what do we hear in music?* Music "does not speak of things, but only of good and bad." These words of Schopenhauer sum up what has been said in many formulations down through the centuries. It would not be exactly true to say that these words express traditional meaning in an undiminished way, but they do pave the way and lead us to what is really meant. "Joy and sorrow" (Wohl und Wehe) are related to the will; the good is the bonum understood as the essential point about willing. The good is willed. Here we have to be warned against moralistic misunderstandings. What is meant is as follows: the being of man is being in the state of happening; man is not simply "there." Man exists as something in a state of becoming—not simply as something growing physically, maturing, gradually moving towards death, but—as a spiritual being—man is also constantly in a state of movement; he "becomes" himself; he is on the way. And that towards which he is moving, to which he is on the way (by his very being—it is impossible for him to do otherwise; man is inwardly underway, he has "not yet arrived," whether he is directly aware of it or not, and whether he likes it or not), the goal to which all this movement strives is the good (even in doing evil the good is intended). We can also say (and the great tradition of Western wisdom has said it!): that to which the insatiable inner striving—this fundamental unrest in which the ultimate drive of our developing existence consists—finally tends is beatitude; before all conscious desire but also in the inner core of conscious desire we want happiness, bliss: that is the good which is our ultimate goal!

What is really meant by this desire and by the process of development itself in which we—in a thousand apparent or real detours—approach this goal, which we have never completely reached, cannot be expressed in words. Neither the goal nor the journey. Augustine says: "'Good'—you hear the word and you take a deep breath, you hear it and you sigh." And he says: the innermost meaning and the richness of meaning to be found in the concept "good"—its full realization—cannot be expressed in human words: "It cannot be said, and it cannot be left unsaid … What are we to do, not speaking and not being silent? Exult! Jubilate! Lift up the non-speaking voice emanating from the joy of your heart …." This "non-speaking voice" (or one of its forms) is: music! — Of course, it is not only the voice of bliss, but (since the good, the aim of the journey is not easily attainable, since it can be "steep" and the target can be missed!) can also be the non-speaking voice of wretchedness, of hopeful nearing the goal, of longing, sadness, despair. Language is not adequate to express the innermost process of our lived being. The process is prior to language, it is in nature (including that of the spirit) and also transcends it; "that is the reason," says Kierkegaard, "that music both precedes and follows language, showing that it is both first and last." Music makes the sphere of silence accessible; in it the soul emerges "naked," so to speak, without the linguistic garment, "that was caught up in all the thorns" (as Paul Claudel says).

I said that the nature of music has been seen like this, in various forms, in the tradition of Western culture; as a speechless expression of joy and sorrow (Wohl und Weh), as expression without words of that innermost process of self-realization which we understand as the growth of the moral person, as desire in all its forms, as love: this is what Plato meant when he said that "music imitates the stirrings of the soul"; or Aristotle: music is similar to the ethical and is associated with it. There are later utterances like that of Kierkegaard, who says that "music, by its own directness, constantly gives expression to immediate reality"; or Schopenhauer: of all the arts, music alone represents the will itself; or Nietzsche, interpreting Wagner: in music nature resounds, "transformed into love."

This means, therefore, that the inner process of human existence is what finds expression in music (as its material, so to speak), where both have in common that they both take place in time. But now, since "music" is not an impersonal objective power but is "made" by very individual musicians, also the following is true: that a thousand different forms of such inner processes can emerge as musical constructions and (since the inner development of the moral person is a natural process which is not exempt from waywardness but is threatened in innumerable ways by danger and destruction) a thousand forms can emerge which are false, twisted and confused. Music can represent shallow self-satisfaction with the easy achievement of the "cheapest" things; the negation of order; despair of the possibility that man's inner development has a goal or that this goal can be reached; it can also be, as in Thomas Mann's *Doctor Faustus*, music of a nihilist, whose stylistic principle is parody and which comes about with "the help of the devil and with hell's fire under the cauldron."

Precisely these possibilities of decadence, the dangers represented by all music-making, have been clear to the ancients, especially Plato and Aristotle, who tried to counter them.

For it is not as if the closeness of music to human existence—as the distinctive characteristic of music—merely means transforming into music the fundamental processes of human existence, genuine and otherwise, right or wrong, insofar as they concern the relationship of the creative artist to his work. It is not as if there were only great and genuine, shallow and spurious music; and it is not as if—on the other side, on the side of the listener—there is merely a neutral relationship of awareness or non-awareness, of applause, of appreciation or non-appreciation. No, the closeness of music to human existence means much more: it means that, because music directly expresses the immediate reality of the fundamental processes of human existence, the listener is addressed and challenged on this same deep level at which fundamental self-realization is achieved. At this level, far deeper than where judgements are formulated, the same strings resonate, with complete immediacy, which resound in the music heard.

Here it becomes clear why and to what extent music is important for human development—or for the contrary—even prior to any conscious preoccupation with education and teaching. Here we see the necessity of reflecting on these very direct influences—as, for instance, Plato and Aristotle did. It is hard for us to understand why these two great Greek philosophers treated of music so seriously and in such detail in their ethical and even in their political writings. According to Plato, music is not only a "means for developing character" but also a tool "for the correct shaping of legal institutions." "It is seen," he says in the "Republic," "as a mere enjoyment and as something which does no harm"; and to think that music is, above all, for the delectation of the listener, whether he has any moral character or not—i.e., whether he is ordered within himself—is a view which Plato, in his late work "Laws," seriously referred to as mendacious. Nowhere can music be changed without serious consequences for the most important laws of the state. According to Plato, that is what a famous Greek musical theorist (Damon) taught, and he (Plato) was convinced that this was correct.

Naturally Plato is not referring to the juridical aspect of the constitution but to the actual inner state of the community with regard to its realization of the good. — And so there is very serious, detailed consideration about which musical forms, and indeed which instruments should be banned from an ordered society; the Middle Ages also—down to the time of Bach—thought of some instruments as not decent. Detail is not important here; naturally, prevailing conditions of the period are at work. The decisive point is to see (and to fix!) the inner link between, on the one hand, the music played and heard by a nation (Volk) and, on the other hand, the inner existence of this nation—just as much today as in the time of Plato!

Of course, we are probably like those for whom, as Plato says, music is seen merely as enjoyable entertainment—whereas, in truth, that mutually conditioning relationship between music—both played and listened to—and the ethos of our inner existence descends all the more readily into pernicious disorder the less we care about genuine order. Our average experience shows, however, that we don't even have a notion that such order is possible, to say nothing of what this order would look like.

If we turn our attention to the empirical reality of life in society and consider how the most trivial mood music, with its cheerful tunes, has become a general public phenomenon—a faithful expression of the banality of cheap self-deception according to which, once in the sphere of inner existence the good has been achieved everything is not so bad and everything is basically "in order"; if we consider what space is claimed by and given over to the rhythms of primitive intoxicating music, music for slaves (as Aristotle said)—where both forms, the music of cheerful tunes and of intoxicating rhythms, find their justification as "entertainment," i.e., as a means to cope with boredom and the emptiness of existence which also, with one element calling on and augmenting the other, have become a general public phenomenon; if we consider that also an incomparably higher formal level of music is sought after and enjoyed as a source of enchantment, of flight from reality, a kind of pseudo-redemption, an ecstasy coming from the outside (as Rilke has said), and that there is music—even great music—that contributes to all of this; if we, finally, consider that parody of creation, the nihilistic music of despair of the great artists exists not only in novels like "Doctor Faustus," so that in all seriousness it can be said that the history of Western music is the "history of the degeneration of the soul"—anyone who, with horror, considers all of these things and has the insight that in music inner existence shows itself (and must show itself) in its nakedness, without veil and without distortion, and the same inner existence itself receives from the same music very direct impulses, both destructive and constructive; anyone who sees and considers all of these things will, with a special and new feeling of happiness reflect that also the music of Johann Sebastian Bach, and precisely that music, still exists!

This represents a challenge to us which cannot be met automatically. It depends on our actual hearing of the real aspect of music. This real aspect must, in the immediacy of our souls, be answered by resounding strings—in a newly kindled clarity, freshness and energy of our inner existence; in the rejection of merely pleasant manifestations of music; in the sober alertness of our vision that does not turn away from the reality of genuine life in favour of premature enjoyment; and in the firmly sustained and unswervingly hopeful turning to the good which satisfies the restlessness of our inner desire and which is the real and sole object of the exultation that resounds in Bach's music with its "non-speaking voice."

This represents a challenge to us which cannot be met automatically. It depends on our actual hearing of the real aspect of music. This real aspect must, in the immediacy of our souls, be answered by resounding strings—in a newly kindled clarity, freshness and energy of our inner existence; in the rejection of merely pleasant manifestations of music; in the sober alertness of our vision that does not turn away from the reality of genuine life in favour of premature enjoyment; and in the firmly sustained and unswervingly hopeful turning to the good which satisfies the restlessness of our inner desire and which is the real and sole object of the exultation that resounds in Bach's music with its "non-speaking voice."

Notes 2

Sleep, celebration and the everyday. — "One of the first symptoms (of nervous illness, neurosis) is usually that one can no longer sleep properly. Here we must be aware that sleep which is sufficient with regard to the length of time can be quite inadequate with regard to quality. Often a change in the nature of one's dreams is the most notice-able thing: they are no longer proper dreams, fairy tale products of a playful, sleepwalking fantasy, but dreary and arid stories in which daily life is simply continued in sleep; the surest sign that it is ... not genuine sleep." This is written in a medical study of nervousness. The first im-portant point is that the working day, if uninterrupted, causes illness. The second point is that this kind of illness is typical of our era. (1946)

"Therefore a well reared person will have the ability to sing well and to dance"—according to Plato in "Laws." The development of fundamental means of expression: it is a relapse into barbarism or rather "progress" into deca-dence that people are no longer capable of fundamental dancing and singing. (1942)

C'est l'amour qui chante. This statement by de Maistre contains something about the essence of song, poetry and music —that they live from a loving impulse. But some-thing is also said about the nature of love itself: namely, that it can only express itself in song, in poetry, in music— in the whirlwind that rages through the organ. (1947)

We do not speak of what we "get from poetry." What poetry produces is the continuation of our awareness of the astonishing aspects of the world. And the real role of genuine philosophizing can be seen in the same way: that our minds are kept alert to the mystery which consists in the fact that there is something we cannot fathom, being that bursts the limits of our thought processes.

"Thinking has its beginnings in image, as in an unconscious state" (Konrad Weiss). — Image is prior to word, and prior to the firmly defined thought is the sensuous, the so to speak less spiritual image. Before the son is Maria. But the word comes from the image; and a word separated from the image is unfruitful. And this relationship, like that between the root and the green plant, is real although the image is the blinder and word is the more seeing element; although word intrinsically is of higher rank, so that it takes its origin from the image as if from an unconscious state. Word separated from this origin and seeking to find its contentment in this self-sufficient "Intellectuality" cheats itself of its own fruit: as long as Orpheus proceeds blindly, Eurydice follows him; but as soon as he—only too confident of success (or: losing faith, which is always something blind)—wants to see with his own independent faculties, his spouse returns to the region of the dead; through his desire to see, he destroys the work that began in blindness. But thought and word must retain in its purity the link with the image, which is relatively blind; without the image, thought and word have no historical effectiveness. It is not the "idea" of bravery, but the image, the symbol (lion, eagle, banner) that has a direct effect; not the conceptually formulated idea of love, but the image of the pelican nourishing its young with its own blood. The Word, the Logos of God, becomes effective in history by being born "of Mary," becoming a visible person; and Mary, although less powerful than her offspring, remains the mediatrix. (1943)

Thomas says, as does Aristotle, that the things that are most obvious in themselves are the things most hidden from our eyes and our soul is to them as the eye of nocturnal birds are to the light of day. — Should it not be the function and the gift of poetry, through magic, as in a magic mirror, to make visible to our eye these things which in themselves are clear and manifest realities? And does not the "obscurity" of the great writers stem from the fact that both they themselves begin to stammer when faced with these realities just as the listeners and readers are too preoccupied with the foreground rational content and thus do not grasp what is mirrored symbolically? It is inevitable that no one perceives what is shining forth as long as he fixes his gaze on the medium through which it shines. This medium is, in the case of poetry, the logical structure and the immediate content of what the verses say. (1943)

Having an organ for poetry seems to be part of human nature. Of course, a person can "live" without the muses, but then he seems to be correspondingly lacking in a sense of higher realities. And it could also be the case that a task presupposes a full and rounded human nature with all its senses, the more demanding it is. A feel for poetry, i.e., the direct knowledge that poetry is a special form of utterance and a special way of grasping the world, seems to me "presupposed" where a person undertakes to interpret Holy Scripture.

If, on the one hand, one sees, with the Church, the writings of the Old and New Testament as "inspired", i.e., as utterances of Holy Spirit, and on the other hand one thinks that poetry is mere play of our free fantasy, something purely invented, a specially shaped and "rhymed" imagination of an individual (the poet)—then naturally the thesis that some of the writings of Holy Scripture are "poetry" appears as unacceptable, even heretical. And biblical interpretation is caught in a dilemma, as happened in the 19th century: either in a purely positivistic way accepting the literal interpretation word for word (which has to end in total absurdity)—or no longer to believe in this absurdity; either "credere quia absurdum" or "non credere quia absurdum."

An idea like that of Augustine of a "total" person who was still able to know directly what poetry meant and had to say about life—Augustine's idea that the story of creation was a sequence of images in which the history of man and his redemption was revealed to the angels had of necessity to seem extremely daring to scholarly exegetes who are concerned exclusively with historical criticism and text analysis—precisely because the feel for poetry has been lost. (1943)

A fundamental idea behind Konrad Weiß's conception of history is that historical concepts, as long as they are replete and rounded, cannot account for Christian existence (and are not in line with the reality of the historical world); they are, instead, to be recognized as Christian and in line with historical reality in that they are not replete, but hungry and needy; not round and smooth, but subject to internal division. The historical and theological reason for this is the "historical Gethsemane," the fact that the Logos, in the Son of Man, went through death.

It would be possible, as has in fact been the case in theological speculation, to try to interpret the incarnation of God as a "replete" and "undivided" concept. One could say that it means bringing the world to a more rounded perfection by the beginning, the foundation of everything, combining with the act of creation so that the circle is completed in the incarnation of the Logos. In a certain sense this is also quite valid, except that the complete historical concept of the incarnation has to include the fact of the shameful crucifixion. And this is where the concept is fractured and split.

Thus the "deficit" and the "gap" are so to speak fundamental phenomena in the history of reality. At the core of genuine historical reality there is the "inner breakdown"; the genuine historical entities are "prior to the objective central core—being built around a gap."

I was very surprised to see recently, in a quite narrow but large and clear reproduction, a detail of the head of Christ from the Isenheim Altarpiece image of the Resurrection of Christ. Anyone who did not know otherwise would not believe that this could be the face of the Christus hovering in truly Baroque style over the grave. While the image as a whole is almost tumultuously dramatic, this face is pure in its structure, wonderfully peaceful, completely well-proportioned, almost like a head by Fra Angelico. This contrast of rest at the centre point while extreme movement is all around it gives the image, so to speak, a new mystical dimension. The lack of repose of the picture is countered by the deep transfigured restfulness, so that "the world" in the image is made round and full. It is an image of Christian history which, ripped to shreds by contrasts and constantly shattered, plays out in the presence of the transfigured Lord. (1942)

The Marian character of great poetry. — Is it not true that theology is closest to poetry in its teaching about Mary? And where poetry becomes theology (and all great poetry is, as also Konrad Weiß says, a theology) it is most likely to be Marian.

The conclusion of Faust. — Dante: the apparition of Mary, with the angel Gabriel as light encircling her head. — "Carefree the rose is open, secure in her hope."

Then there is the theological symbolism for Mary.

The Litany of the Blessed Virgin—in contrast to all other prayers which are similar in form—is clearly poetic. Expressions like "You mystic rose," "You tower of ivory" are poetic in nature. The epistles relating to Marian feasts: Mary is "wisdom," which is similar to the Word. — In the doctrine about Mary, at least in the great Mariological tradition, a rationalistically narrow principle of identity has to be relinquished. Mary is at the same time the mother of Christ and our mother; she is the bride of Christ (but the Church is also the bride of Christ) and at the same time the wisdom at play in God's presence from the beginning. (1945)

"Functional music." — "Almost exclusively Bach wrote functional music, some of which makes up the greatest works in music literature." This was written by Paul Höffer, the composer, in an essay on the situation of contemporary music. Höffer's opinion is that, for instance, for a Party proclamation or any other similar politically representative event an opening piece of music should be specially commissioned for the occasion. In this way there will again be living, new music.

Against this idea it should be said that Bach's music is great music not simply because it is "functional" but because—leaving aside Bach's genius—it is (or was) functional in the context of worship. Through establishing a new link with worship a new kind of music could be produced, perhaps. (1946)

III

The sacraments work causally,
giving meaning through signs.

Thomas Aquinas

The Greater World
Christmas Meditation on Justice and Peace
(1952)

That which is quite simply past cannot really be celebrated. A day of celebration and a day of commemoration
are different things. A celebration implies that what is
being celebrated is really relevant to one's present existence, illuminating and elevating it—not in a purely historical reflection but in its immediate living reality. People
have always seen it in this light when dealing with the celebration of a feast: the enrichment of life originates from
somewhere beyond the human.

Where this is no longer experienced and such an experience is no longer possible, to that extent the possibility
of celebrating ceases to exist. Despite appearances and no
matter what efforts are made, nothing can give the lie to
this simple fact. Decorations with lights and shepherd
songs, the lovely excitement with surprises and gifts, the
warmest openness to joy, even the deeper readiness to
help one another: all of this does not succeed in making a
day a real celebration. A feast does not come about by
human arrangement. Only the gods, as Plato knew and
said, are able to create a day of celebration. — Anyone
who ponders this may be horrified to realize how much

the human existence of our contemporaries has lost the sense of celebration. And this of necessity.

But this does not at all call for a song of lamentation. Nor is it justified on this occasion, *in hac sacratissima nocte*, to speak of the "gods."

Let us leave aside the poetry, customs, emotionality and business—all that is secondary, all the elements that are meaningful, respectable and perhaps even indispensable. Let us ponder the intransitory transcendent event which is the only basis for celebrating Christmas. If we ponder the totally unidyllic "fact" that has taken place in the innermost core of the world and is hidden in the theological term "incarnation," we may, as Dante in his *Purgatorio* is caught in the violent and painful clutches of the angel / eagle, feel overpowered and thrown into an inaccessible sphere; we may be drawn into the undertow of the unfathomable and incomprehensible, the simply improbable and utopian. Except that it is, at the same time, real in the highest sense! And if we then look up and look back we find, furthermore, that we have not left "our" world and have not landed in a separate sphere beyond our world. It becomes clear that precisely this immeasurable incomprehensible sphere is where human existence is lived—as always and also in the present moment in time. We see likewise the "improbable" destiny meant for man, what he could be, what he was designed for and to what he is called.

With regard to the situation of justice, for example (one gives to the other what is owing to him, gives him what is "his"), it may seem at first sight that this is completely within the world of our experience. And how could metaphysics or even theology come into play where there is simply a question of giving to another what is his due? The answer: if being just means giving everyone what is his then clearly this presumes that there is such a thing as "his," i.e., that something is due to the person I am dealing with. But the question is: on what basis is anything due to someone? It is not just paying back a loan or paying the sale price of something but also respecting a person's life, his physical integrity, his freedom. What is the basis for all of this being his due—and so irrevocably that anyone who deprives him of these things does incomparably more damage to himself than to his partner? This Socratic wisdom really comes to light when it is taken literally: the perpetrator of injustice is "more to be pitied," more profoundly disfigured and wounded than the person who suffers the injustice. Should such an absolute claim to one's due be based on something purely empirical? Can "what is his" as the presupposition of justice be taken seriously? Is justice itself conceivable as the "nature of the soul through which we are the servant of no one except God alone" (as Augustine puts it); is all of this inalienable humanity quite comprehensible—above all, achievable—if man's nature is not understood in his supra-empirical "improbability," residing in that greater sphere of which we reassure ourselves in celebrating today's feast?

We must pose this question even more insistently if we focus on the concept of peace, which has indeed become "improbable." The barest mutual agreement, the mere going along with one another, just getting on: all of this, which is very difficult and hardly to be expected would seem to us highly desirable, even though we are in no position to speak of concordia, unanimity, unity. And then even harmony is still not peace (according to the ancients). Of course, they see peace as "coming," as the future; Isaias's sentence about the fruit of justice being peace—opus justitiae pax—is in the future tense.

And so in the opinion of the ancients what is the distinction between unity and peace? And who would not be filled with the deepest mistrust to see some private individual appear with the claim that he has for us a "new" teaching about justice, about peace, and about the essence of man? One of the great masters of Western Christendom has given the following answer: peace includes the notion of unity, but unity does not include the notion of peace. It is possible for men to be one with one another without being one with themselves. Only when both coincide— the inner rightness of the person and agreement with one another—only then is there "peace" in the undiminished sense. But because no one can be one with himself if he does not, with all his strength, want what is right—no one can turn to injustice without some kind of resistance and therefore without discord in his own bosom—there can be peace only between the "good," whereas unity is possible where there is badness.

I am trying to imagine how purely "abstract" such ideas must seem to the unprepared reader, how much they must seem to come from a far-off "moral" world. It must be admitted that even this aspiration which he can say is "unreal" but not really inconceivable falls infinitely far short of the "peace of God" of which the sacred book of Christianity says it surpasses all understanding.

And why speak about all of this? Because, so it seems to me, it is necessary from time to time for man to ponder the utmost limits of what he can be. Again and again to realize that these utmost limits are not pure utopia—this is where we can find the meaning and possibility of celebrating real feasts, especially that of the present day, which says that human possibilities are of divine proportions.

Comments on the Missionary Situation of the Church in Germany (1936)

Recently a book by Stefan Gilson appeared in Paris under the title "For a Catholic Regime." In this book, according to a report in *Hochland*, especially the Catholics themselves are told about their true tasks: "They should not just, amongst themselves, be triumphal in celebrating again and again the excellence of their principles but realize that the world in which they live has become a missionary country and that they are to set to work as spiritual missionaries. This idea, in both its negative and positive aspects, is relevant not only for France but also for Germany.

The Church's mission in Germany has not yet been fulfilled. The process of Christianizing the German people is not yet finished; the situation of the Church in Germany is a missionary situation.

If we admit this we are compelled to accept some weighty consequences. We must accept that the work of the Church in Germany must continue to function with missionary categories and presuppositions. And this is very significant.

It means, above all, that the eternal ideas of Christianity need to be fundamentally rethought and newly formulated, taking into consideration the spiritual reality of the people to be missionized. Here the categories must come into force which, according to the express wishes of Pius X (Mission Encyclical), are to apply to all missions and in line with which the Indian Mission, for example, tries to express fundamental Christian truths using concepts drawn from the ancient Indian books of wisdom.

The task of Christianizing Germany therefore includes the other task of "translating" Christian truth and reality into German. This latter task—vigorously undertaken especially by German mysticism of the High and Late Middle Ages, then broken off or further developed in an anti-Church sense by the Reformation—must today, now that the Counter Reformation has ended, be energetically resumed. It hardly needs to be said that we are here not talking about a variant of Christianity based on a corruption of eternal Christian truths.

It is well known that the classical missionary speech, St. Paul's speech in the Areopagus, did not begin with any kind of self-defense but with the words: "Men of Athens! I find you in every sense God fearing. For as I walked around and observed your sacred monuments I found an altar which bore the inscription: to an unknown God. Well, what you honor without knowing it is the God I now proclaim to you." And the following famous sentences of the 1 Corinthians (9, 19ff.] express the principles of all missionary activity: "So though I am not a slave to any man I have made myself the slave of everyone so as to win as many as I could. I made myself a Jew to the Jews, to win the Jews; that is, I who am not a subject of the Law made myself a subject of the Law to those who are the subjects of the Law, to win those who are subject to the Law. To those who have no Law, I was free of the Law myself (though not free from God's law, being under the law of Christ) to win those who have no Law. For the weak I made myself weak. I made myself all things to all men in order to save some at any cost; and I still do this, for the sake of the gospel, to have a share in its blessings."

Perhaps it is also necessary to say that not only this core missionary attitude of St. Paul but also its application to the here and now has nothing to do with the notion of a purely "reactive" Christianity that always fits in so as always to seem "modern" and "contemporary." Missions are a fundamental task of the Church. "Missionary" Christianity and "reactive" Christianity are oceans apart. It is not a question of the prestige of Christianity but of winning for Christ the nations to which the Church was sent in the first place.

From the missionary situation of the Church in Germany something else follows which is also very important. It is the need to highlight, very energetically, the primary and central truths and realities of Christianity by contrast with what is only secondary. (Naturally, this need does not follow first and foremost from the missionary situation. It is based on what is essential and is prior to all external setting of goals; but through the missionary situation the need becomes heightened and acutely pressing.) What is really primary in Christian faith and life is the mystery of the Trinity and redemption through Jesus Christ, made present in the sacraments of the Church, above all in the sacrifice and sacrificial meal in the Mass. But now, if even for the Christian believer this primary reality of Christianity is obscured and veiled by a superabundance of what is secondary, how slight must be the prospects for a non-Christian of seeing the true core of Christianity and thus coming into contact with the force it radiates? There is an obvious and therefore much practiced but extremely dangerous answer to the question about the present situation of Christianity: precisely to strengthen and develop the secondary aspects. This kind of answer is the exact opposite of what is really necessary. It derives from a kind of laziness which shuns the "new beginning" which is the task facing every missionary. It would be like the life force of a tree being completely given to the growth of one particular branch instead of returning to the trunk and promoting the growth of new branches alongside and above the first.

The shift from apologetics to missionary work with all that follows requires considerable spiritual energy in resisting one's own, so to speak, natural tenacity. This shift—which first must be a matter of mind rather than organization—requires a spiritual energy similar to the kind shown by Paul when as a missionary in Antioch he defended the principles of the mission to the heathens against the conservative attitude of the wavering Peter, "opposing him to his face."

The German Church, in the present "missionary situation," will have to demonstrate its creativity above all by itself manifesting what Augustine calls the "loving openness" of Paul's demands along with the "loving humility" characterized by Peter's response.

*

Karl Thieme answered this with an Open Letter expressing above all the following ideas:

The term "missionary situation" is a "wrong description" of our position, since a missionary is confronted with non-Christians, whereas in Germany the believer is confronted with anti-Christians or at least ex-Christians who have become indifferent. One must not be manoeuvred into the position of being "a German to the Germans," just as it is impossible to be a "heretic to the heretics." "We are in no way required, like the missionary, to tell heathens about Jesus—who as yet they know nothing about him—but as Our Lord predicted in his parting speeches (Matthew 24, 8–13) we will have to persist in withstanding the temptations of false teaching (verse 11) and lovelessness (verse 12)." There is also an "uncritical missionary zeal" which forgets the words of the Lord that what is holy is not to be given to dogs, and pearls are not to be cast before swine.

My answer to this was as follows:

Wrong descriptions, we would agree, can be very dangerous in that they suggest objectively unfounded points of view and presuppositions. But I do not think that "missionary situation" and "missionizing" are false descriptions of what I mean. Your objection is based on a narrower meaning of these words which, however, in normal parlance have an "accepted" more general meaning ...

It is a fact that today (but not just beginning from today, although it has become clear that the present day is the end of, say, a hundred-year-long development) it is possible for someone in Germany, "in good faith" and "with a clear conscience," to be an non-Christian, even an anti-Christian, without having to be an ex-Christian—especially if he is still young. This amounts to nothing more than saying that the general public atmosphere has lost its strictly Christian character, so that the individual, in order to be a non-Christian, does not have to become isolated and make a special effort to resist the binding and normative general consciousness. According to the measure that this possibility (of being, with a clear conscience, a non-Christian) is increased by these factors, by the same measure the genuine "missionary situation" is constituted (almost even to the point of being a real "mission to the heathens" in the strict sense).

In response to your reference to Matthew 24, 8ff. I would like to say the following: apart from the perhaps in the strictest sense eschatological meaning of this text I do not think that hardship, false teaching exclude the missionary situation. In fact, they are the very "eternal" ingredients of every genuine missionary situation (since Constantine almost all martyrs are missionaries).

To sum up my two answers so far: first, the Church, in its teaching role in Germany as in nearly all European countries, is faced with a large contingent of non-Christians who have influence in shaping public consciousness and who "know nothing about Christ"; second, the interpretation of the present situation by reference to Matt. 24, 8ff. does not at all exclude seeing it as a missionary situation.

Furthermore, naturally there is no such thing as a German culture separate from Christianity; naturally the "old-German books of wisdom" have been partly influenced by Christianity; and naturally even today's non-Christians live from the inheritance of this culture influenced by Christianity. But against this there is the fact that the Church, in its teaching role, does not reach large parts of the population because it speaks a language which for them is incomprehensible. To avoid misunderstandings, some points in this sentence require clarification. First, I am not here referring to Latin as the language of worship but to the language used for teaching; and here I do not mean "language" merely as vocabulary but as a way of speaking and as everything that—in images and symbols, in personal presentation etc.—serves to reveal and clarify the Christian message. And by the "teaching Church" I am not referring to the ultimate teaching authority of the Church but to all those who as preachers, catechists, and writers, in direct contact with the people convey the Christian truths. The "teaching Church" in this sense is made up of all those who have been given the power to shape—or even twist—the language in which the teaching is communicated. And my thesis is as follows: the customary language (in that general sense) of this "teaching Church" is quite unsuitable and incapable of making the content of Christian teaching accessible to a broad sector of the German population, even if they were to hear it.

I know quite well that here there are quite different divisive and negative factors at play, and not only human ones. But it is not our duty to identify only deafness and obduracy. Our task is to proclaim the Christian reality again and again, ever more clearly and always in a new way.

In my book on Courage I have already said that the proclaiming of truth seems to include the duty of continually shaping language anew. The thesis concerning this has, I think, like everything connected with "language," two sides. Language is always a sign "of something" "for someone"; it is always the presentation of something and at the same time it is communication. And the shortcomings of language in the teaching Church we are concerned with here are twofold: first, this "language" is unsatisfactory as presentation of the essentially Christian truths; and second, it is inadequate as communication. Correction of the first deficit comes through our reflecting on what is essential. Correction of the second deficit consists in (as I have formulated it in my "Comments") rethinking and giving a new formulation of the eternal truths of Christianity, keeping in mind the spiritual reality of the people to be missionized.

There remains your objection to the concept of "translating" Christianity into German. I shall not go into the historical aspect of the question, since that would inevitably lead to a debate which, on principle, would have no end. But I would like, using some quite general remarks, to show that your opinion on this point (it is above all your opinion, since it is intrinsically impossible that the German teaching Church should only now become a German to the Germans) is based on an unacceptable oversimplification.

The Christianizing of a people is analogous to the Christianizing of the individual, i.e., to the union achieved between nature and the supernatural in the individual person. But while the relationship between nature and the supernatural is indeed "theoretically" and essentially an "harmonious" relationship (gratia non destruit, sed supponit et perficit naturam), it is almost never directly "harmonious" in practice and existentially—for the concrete, historically unique individual case. The concrete "nature" is not at all merely the "presupposition" for the unfolding of the supernatural. It is also a hindrance to this development. Conversely, the unfolding of the supernatural can induce an estrangement of "nature" from itself. And this can happen (a further complication!) not really by virtue of the supernatural "as such," but by virtue of—or the lack of—the "natural" freedom to give shape to the life of the person who has been raised to the supernatural order. In an analogous way the Christianizing of a people can induce an alienation from the natural substance that is peculiar to it. I repeat: such an alienation of the self would not be the expression of an essential relationship between nature and the supernatural; it is rather the concrete existential result of natural historical conditions. (It is therefore not permissible to interpret the Christianizing of the Germanic people simply as a result of an essentially harmonious relationship between nature and the supernatural; that is the basic error of all utterances about the theme "the Germanic and the Christian" which presuppose that there is harmony; likewise it is not possible to "explain" the inner history of a saintly existence in such a simplistic way.)

There is the further complication that with regard to the special historical case of the Christianizing of the German people the mutual tension between nature and the supernatural is accompanied by the other tension—the German/Latin tension—which for the Romanic people is largely non-existent. And then a final complication: the twofold possibility of self-alienation from the natural substance of one's own people is a quite particular danger for the German people—much more so than for the French—so that the German who is alienated from himself is "typically German" precisely in this self-alienation. It follows clearly from this that if there is the possibility of such self-alienation [as an historical concomitant phenomenon but not as an essential consequence of Christianization] there is also the possibility of a "return" to the natural substance of one's people. And such a "return," if it does not belittle and exclude the Christian, would give more meaningful expression to the essential relationship between nature and the supernatural (just as in the individual person the "harmony" of both spheres is based in his essence). The formulation which you have rejected and which is wrong (and which I have not employed)—"to become a German to the Germans"—would give expression, even if inaccurately, to something which is not at all self-contradictory; it would express the idea that it is the historically concrete combining of nature and the supernatural, occurring in the Christianizing of a people, which induces a self-alienation from the people's natural substance, and that there can be a return from this self-alienation. (We must note, of course, that not every factual aspect of the life of the people is an essential expression of their people's substantial creative powers.)

I think, in fact, that after German mysticism and since the Reformation and the Counter Reformation the very strong movement of "translation" into German has been broken off. I am convinced that this movement had to be broken off for the sake of the infinitely more important preservation in their purity of the substantial transcendent truths of Christianity. (This does not mean that all the details of "process of repression" were acceptable.) But I think that today it is again both possible and necessary to resume and develop the abandoned project. Contemporary German Christianity could learn a great deal, precisely for this task, from the Old German book of wisdom, The Heliand, which is largely unknown to it. The same could be said of Meister Eckhart. We only need to compare with the terminology of our text books and tracts his "language" as a teacher: "Every time I preach I speak of distance and I say that the human being must become free of himself and of all things. But a second thing is that we should be built back again into the simply good—which is God. Thirdly, we should remember the great nobility which God has laid in the soul and that through it man enters into the wonderful life of God. Fourthly, with regard to the purity of the divine nature: the clarity of the divine nature is beyond all expression."

On the TV Transmission of Mass (1953)

1

On the basis of the historical process which we call "secularization" there is, above all, an increasing devitalization of our natural religious notions. We are dealing with something which is even worse and more hopeless than "dechristianization" because the hand with which we can grasp what is really Christian seems to be withering. On the other hand, because the process is not formally and directly "dechristianizing" it succeeds all the more easily and unnoticeably in establishing itself within Christianity itself.

The concept "sign" in the sense of a real symbol is, for example, not a concept peculiar to Christianity alone; but no one who is unable to experience the meaning of this concept is able to understand and experience what a sacrament is. But what is true of the concept of "sign" is similarly true of the concept of "sacrifice"—which Thomas assigns to the sphere of "natural law"—and is also true of the concept of "sacred act."

2

Now with regard to the TV transmission of Mass, it seems to me to presuppose on the one hand that the live sense of a "sacred act" is essentially watered down; on the other hand—and above all—through such transmissions the process of dilution is promoted to the point of no return.

It belongs to the essence of the sacred act that there is line separating it from the profane sphere—from the market place and the street. But it is precisely this line which is crossed and deleted by TV transmissions. It is even declared as non-existent, so that the real name for what happens here is "profanation."

The argument which is sometimes advanced that Mass can be worthily celebrated in dance-halls, concentration camps, etc., is missing the central point at issue, because in all of these cases the "line" is a reality—if only one created by the silent reverence of those who "stand around" and share the celebration.

In the case of the TV Mass, however, this barrier is destroyed in two ways: first, the transmission puts the image of sacred act out into the profane sphere—onto the street, into the market place, and into every situation of everyday life without exception; second, processes relating to public curiosity and boredom penetrate into the space of the sacred action.

We should not look at the vehicle of the transmission, the television system, purely abstractly—for instance, as the mere enabling of an optical and acoustical transmission from one place to many other places. Seen from a concretely sociological point of view, television is an instrument of mass entertainment—a fact which gives more weight to the argument that a TV transmission of Mass is opposed to the sacred character of the act. The unthinking way in which (in an approved report about the Paris transmissions) avoidance of monotony by change of "décor" is spoken about is an extremely unsettling confirmation of the fact that completely foreign categories are at play here.

3

Besides, not only the "sacred act" in the stricter sense of celebratory worship is affected here. There are also natural "mysteries" which a healthy mind protects in a silence inspired by reverence and modesty. Anyone who dares to photograph the face of a person while he is immersed in prayer or while as a believer he receives the Body of Christ, and not by chance and in passing (as may happen sometimes on special occasions) but intentionally as part of a plan; and anyone who—as seems common practice in the Paris "Television Chapel"—presumes to expose the faithful to the camera in such a situation must consider that he is thereby committing an act of profanation which differs only in degree from the publicizing by film of a birth, a death, and an act of reproduction.

4

All of this in no way implies that Christian preaching and missionizing should not be allowed to use all technical means, including television. On the contrary, they must be used. But missionizing essentially means introducing people to faith and mystery. But nowhere in the history of Church has the direct presentation of the mystery to the uninitiated been seen as a possible form of missionizing. Television does, undoubtedly, present new possibilities for missionizing, but transmission of the celebration of Mass is not one of them.

5

It has been said that we can expect that from the televised Mass the faithful will gain a "strengthening of their religious sense." Once it has become quite clear that sacramental participation at Mass cannot be achieved through a TV transmission, all that we can assume is left is assistance or intensification of "mental" participation. But this assumption seems highly problematic. Plato said that even writing, although it is a means of recording and preserving things, amounts to a weakening of the person's ability to remember. And it is a well-established fact that the technical aids to seeing and the increased provision of visual material has weakened the intensity of our seeing in an alarming way. It is more than questionable whether the TV transmission of Mass brings about, on average, an increase of inner participation or whether the person who is sick or otherwise disabled— and the case is cited again and again—would not enjoy more intense participation in the sacred act by reading the prayers of the Mass or by focusing on it internally. It is a primary duty of religious education to make believers capable of such inner participation. Not only can this result not be expected from the seeming "help" offered by the TV Mass, but on the contrary the danger is that it will be thwarted.

*

Still, the decisive counter-argument remains that of "profanation." I think that one of the most convincing and positive results of the liturgical renewal movement is that this is seen as the reason why straightforward people reject the TV Mass and, as I know from numerous conversations and discussions, why it is also the instinctive answer, above all, of the large majority of young academic people.

Priesthood and Sacrificial Worship (1953)

1

To have a special private opinion about priesthood makes no sense. Anyone concerned with the truth in this matter will try to listen to and weigh up the only legitimate information on this subject, namely, the information which has the same origin as does the priesthood itself. He will not call on the clever ideas of the critical minds but on the great traditions and on those who are "wise in divine things."

No one becomes a priest by virtue of his own decision nor by virtue of appointment by a community. Training, study, ascetic preparation can be indispensable as a presupposition, but they are never a cause. All this is obvious. There are no priests except on the basis of consecration, i.e., on the basis of communication of a supernatural power.

Since this is the case, subjective opinions are irrelevant in this sphere—which applies even more, the more "interesting" they are—if they claim to be more than or other than an interpretation of that traditional knowledge about the priesthood that has been handed down along with the priesthood itself.

The aim of the following remarks is to attempt a contribution to such an interpretation.

2

"Priests are consecrated with a view to performing the sacrament of the Body of Christ." That sentence is from the *Summa theologica* of St. Thomas. It says concisely and accurately what a priest really is and in what his function consists.

Sacrificial worship is the reason why there are priests, and therefore anyone incapable of knowing the meaning of sacrificial worship and experiencing it is thereby in no position to understand the essence and role of priesthood. This statement is, I think, of the utmost relevance today.

What is at the heart of the "secularization" process, which is observable everywhere, is not that the binding force of ethical norms is slackening, nor that "religion" is losing its power to shape public life, nor that the political and social importance of the Church is vanishing. Nor is "dechristianization" of life, a term which only too readily springs to mind, any nearer the mark. What is happening fundamentally is not that we are going blind in a way which affects our human existence but not our formally Christian existence. Rather, we are losing the ability to see that experiencing sacrificial worship is at all meaningful and that it could even been necessary. As a result, people are no longer able to say why the priest—and not only the Christian priest—has an indispensable and even meaningful role to play in human society.

Blindness of this kind is a quite serious threat to Christianity itself. And even priests can have this blindness. This is evident in many ways. For example, we often hear that the role of the priest seems more and more to be taken over—according to certain sociological laws—by other professions: the doctor, the teacher, the psychotherapist. Whether this is said as a mere observation, or with regret, or with satisfaction, it is always based on the same opinion: that the real role of the priest is something other than that of sacrificial worship. It would not occur to anyone to think or say that this latter function could be taken over by a non-priest.

That is not to say that the role of the priest should or could be limited to performing the sacrificial function (and dispensing the sacraments, which indeed are nothing but the different forms of applying the sacrifice and sharing in it). Naturally, the priest will always be active in teaching, leading, and exercising the ministry. In this, not only his spiritual function but the whole of his concrete humanity—his strengths and his weaknesses—will play a part according to the measure of his personal vitality, the knowledge and skill he has acquired, his tact, and his natural abilities as a whole.

However, it is necessary to distinguish between what the priest does and his "priestly activity." Only the latter concerns us here. Priestly activity, in the strict sense, is purely the performance of sacrificial worship. But according to Thomas there is another "secondary" but likewise priestly activity: the preparation of the people for sharing in the sacrifice. This distinction is not meant as a vague description but lays the claim to mapping out the ground and thereby characterizing and encompassing the totality of the priestly function.

3

There is nothing less surprising than that the criteria for judging the priest must become confused because of blindness to the meaning of sacrifice. We could hardly expect it to be otherwise.

If therefore real priestly activity consists in performing the sacrifice, who, then, is an "outstanding" priest? What weight, what meaning can be attributed to all the usual terms we use—and their opposites—like "competent," "important," "excellent," "open to the world," "progressive"?

Surely there are good and bad priests. However, it must be accepted that the priesthood as such, proprie et principaliter, is not affected by this—just as, as the ancients said, it does not matter whether the pipe through which the water flows into the well is made of silver or of lead. The pouring out of salvation and grace happens in any case—even if by "bad" we mean not the lack of intelligence and ability but the lack of purity, goodness, piety. In such a case, of course, the priest would not be a living and devoted instrument, like the hand, but a lifeless instrument like an axe (both the distinction and the example are taken from the *Summa theologica*). But even the lifeless instrument will produce the effect: through the God-Man, the one who really performs the sacrifice and who can never fail.

When it is a question of the "secondary" activity of the priest there can very well be failure and distinction, namely, in the preparation of the people for participating in the sacrifice. Here his activity is needed with all his vitality and his inner spiritual and moral force. This is, therefore, the real sphere in which evaluation, praise and criticism—above all self-criticism—find their place.

This applies particularly to that kind of activity of the priest which cannot really be called "priestly activity." Performance of the sacrifice, of itself, is not subject to criticism, but the actions of a priest, the more they are removed from this internal sphere, have to be demonstrably in line with proper standards. The further it is removed from the vocation, the office, and dignity of the priesthood the more it is necessary to show proof of personal competence and ability. Of course, it is one of the specific temptations of the holder of office to take scant notice of something so obvious. That should not mean that secular functions should not devolve on the priest—on both the institution and the individual. Who would care to pass judgment on what the political bishops of Clodowick's era, the Benedictine gardeners and bee keepers in the early years in the West, the priestly scholars, teachers, founders and leaders of all eras, "really" should have been doing? However, these are activities which are, on principle, subject to critical criteria which differ from those of proper priestly activity.

4

If Thomas's words about the two kinds of priestly function adequately express the substance of established tradition, and the whole duty of the priesthood is to be described as the performance of the sacrifice on the one hand and, on the other hand, as the training of the faithful to participate in the sacrifice, what then makes someone a "good" priest and when would he be failing in his duty? The answer is almost implied in the question.

First, the "good," the truly priestly priest will endeavour, in performing the sacrifice, not to be merely a dead instrument but to be "like a living hand." The only way this can happen is that, in the contemplative engagement with Holy Scripture and the utterances of the Church in its prayers and sacrifice, he immerses himself, with all the strength of his mind and his dedication, into the mystery of the God-Man and His sacrifice. Anyone who is aware of the workload of a priest in a major city can only be hesitant in expressing such a demand. Yet here we are dealing with the root and inner core of priestly existence: namely, that the sacrifice does not only take place objectively but is experienced in the depth of the person. Otherwise how could we speak of the performance of the sacrifice as of a truly human act?

Here we have the crucial presupposition regarding the second requirement which the "good" priest must satisfy: namely, that he lead the people to share in the sacrifice.

He can fail in this "secondary" task in two ways. Either it could be that a priest does not see or acknowledge the preparation of the people for sharing in the sacrifice as the meaning of his pastoral activity or it could mean that he has lost sight of this goal. The diversity of "religious events" and the themes dealt with in the Sunday sermon is, in every way, a disturbing symptom.

Another way of failing to carry out the priestly office could consist not in denying the goal but in not pursuing it vigorously enough. The aim is affirmed but the means are ineffective, too weak, or simply wrong. It could be that what is lacking in the priest's effectiveness is the power to motivate and convince. That can have a hundred different causes which have to do with ability, temperament, and training in theology, pedagogy and preaching. This would mean failure in carrying out his essentially priestly role only if it arose from his not affirming strongly enough and realizing within himself the special sharing in the sacrifice of the God-Man which comes with that office—if, therefore the reason was a lack of spirituality. A spiritual priest is not just a "pious" priest and is certainly not the same as an "intelligent," "cultivated," "broad-minded" priest. Spirituality means that not only a person's ability to love but precisely the power of his mind focuses, with all the insatiable urge within it, on the divine mysteries, so that every utterance of the knowing spirit is flooded and inflamed by them—in such a way, however, that the thinking and expression loses nothing in regard to accuracy, sobriety, penetration, objectivity. In a word: spirituality is the fruit of contemplation.

As everyone knows, priests are criticized in many ways, and naturally not every criticism deserves to be answered and taken seriously. Sometimes it seems that not only the criticism but also the kind of answer given is based on the fact that one no longer knows what priesthood really is, what it really does and therefore in what its failure consists.

With regard to the more or less important criticisms directed at the thousand manifestations of human weakness, it may be sufficient to ask for a level of fraternal understanding on the one hand and active self-criticism on the other – things which are also indispensable for us in our normal social intercourse.

It would be different if the criticism was: the priest is lacking in all understanding of the meaning of the sacrifice and for this reason does not do justice to his role in helping people to participate in the sacrifice. Such a criticism has incomparable weight because it strikes at the heart of the priesthood. And if such a criticism is heard, even if only as a worry and an impression, it should be given the most serious consideration.

Comments on the Lord's Supper Tract in the *Summa theologica* (1937)

1

Anyone who is used to seeing in Thomas Aquinas the man who, in the High Middle Ages, was co-responsible for founding and, so to speak, introducing the forms of Eucharistic celebration which are separate from the Mass liturgy, can only be astonished and surprised after studying the Lord's Supper Tract in the *Summa theologica*. In the whole of this tract there is not one thing that points in this direction. This is quite strange.

The fundamental thrust of the eleven comprehensive Questions of the Tract is quite simply this: that the Mass is where the sacrament of the altar takes place; and when there is mention of "usus" and "ritus" it is always and exclusively the Mass that is referred to. "This sacrament is simultaneously sacrifice and sacrament," hoc sacramentum simul est sacrificium et sacramentum. The emphasis on the word "simul" affects all statements in the Tract.

2

There is hardly any further need for stressing that for Thomas the people's communion at Mass is taken for granted and seems to him the only meaningful possibility (apart from communion of the sick, of course); as a consequence he interprets the Mass liturgy itself—above all, the prayers from the Our Father to the prayer for peace—as the preparation, not only of the priest but explicitly also of the people, for receiving the Lord's Supper. Today's ritual (with the Confiteor, etc.) was not introduced until the late Middle Ages.

In two Articles of the Tract Thomas gave a brief explanation of the Mass liturgy, of the prayers and the actions (quae dicuntur, quae aguntur). In the first of these we read: "The part that follows (the prayer Nobis quoque peccatoribus) relates to the receiving of the sacrament; first the people are prepared to receive it." It is important to see what Thomas considers the way this preparation should happen: first, "through the prayer shared by the whole people, the prayer of the Lord, in which we pray that we may receive our daily bread"; second, "the people are prepared with the kiss of peace …; for this sacrament is the sacrament of unity and peace." "Then follows the receiving of the sacrament; the priest receives it first, and then he gives it to the others."

3

We have just quoted from Thomas's explanation of the Mass (which, by the way, is not in every respect the most profound of his writings) the statement that the Lord's Supper is the sacrament of unity and peace. This is not something formulated by Thomas simply as a casual explanation of the kiss of peace. Instead, we are dealing with an idea which is fundamental to his whole teaching about the Lord's Supper. "The Lord's Supper is the sacrament of

Church unity," Eucharistia est sacramentum ecclesiasticae unitatis. Statements of this kind occur frequently. The unity of the Mystical Body and unity with the Mystical Body, without which there is no salvation, is part of the core reality, the "res" of this sacrament: res hujus sacramenti est unitas corporis mystici, sine qua non potest esse salus. "The 'res' of this sacrament is twofold: one (res) is meant and included, namely Christ himself; the other is meant but not included, namely the Mystical Body of Christ, which is the communion of saints. Everyone, therefore, who receives this sacrament is giving a sign that he is one with Christ and included in his members." "Unity with the Mystical Body is the fruit of receiving the real body." The reason for establishing this sacrament is that it should be nourishment through becoming one with Christ and his members, just as nourishment is one with the person it nourishes." While the word Communion (communion) in modern times almost exclusively refers to the union of the individual with Christ (seen, so to speak, as an individual) Thomas uses this word mainly to refer to the unity of the Mystical Body into which the individual is incorporated by receiving the Lord's Supper. Here he quotes words taken from the works of John of Damascus: "communion" is said "because in it we are in communion with Christ both by participating in His flesh and His divinity and by being a community and unity with one another." Thomas takes in its literal sense the Pauline idea that "we, the many who share in the one bread and the one chalice, are one bread and one body" (1 Cor. 10, 17). And to the objection that in the animal sacrifices in the Old Testament the Passion of the Lord is much more expressively signified than in the bread and wine, he replies with, among other things, the answer that these sacrifices cannot meaningfully function as signs referring to the unity of the Church—ad significandam ecclesiasticam unitatem.

Thomas sees the idea of the Mystical Body of Christ likewise as the basis for the prayers for the dead spoken in canon of the Mass, i.e., directly in the celebration of the Lord's Supper: "The Lord's Supper is the sacrament of the unity of the whole Church." That is why, precisely in this sacrament more than the others, there is mention of everything that concerns the salvation of the whole Church.

4

The words in which Thomas sets out the relationship between baptism and the Lord's Supper are in some ways surprising and worthy of particular attention. Thomas sees in the Lord's Supper "simply the most sublime" of all the sacraments. All the other sacraments are seen in relation to the Lord's Supper as their goal. Thus he says of baptism that in it man receives authority to go to the Lord's Supper; he is prepared by it for the Lord's Supper. "Through baptism man is oriented towards the Lord's Supper. Thus the small children, precisely by virtue of baptism, are being led by the Church in the direction of the Lord's Supper, and just as they are believers by virtue of the Church's faith so also they yearn for the Lord's Supper by virtue of the aims set by the Church." "The sacrament of the Lord's Supper, although received later than baptism is, however, prior to it with regard to its purpose; therefore it is meaningful that it was established earlier" (than baptism). "No one has grace before receiving this sacrament (the Lord's Supper) unless on the basis of the desire and the intention to receive it, and indeed, either— as is the case with adults—on the basis of one's own desire, or—as with small children—on the basis of the desire and intention of the Church.

5

There are misunderstandings without number which arise from translating the Latin word "spiritualis" with the German word "geistlich." "Spiritualis" includes not only the meaning of both "geistig" and "geistlich" but it also includes "that which refers to the Holy Spirit."

The distinction between the manducatio sacramentalis and the manducatio spiritualis, between the sacramental and the mental receiving of the Lord's Supper, is found in the *Summa theologica* in a very significant context. But for Thomas the manducatio spiritualis means something entirely different from what we mean by "spiritual communion." In our parlance, "spiritual communion" means, negatively, "non-bodily" communion; positively, it means the "inner desire" for the genuine bodily sacramental receiving of the Lord's Supper. But how does Thomas see this distinction? "In receiving communion two things are to be considered: the sacrament itself and its fruit. The perfect way to receive this sacrament is to receive in such a way that also the fruit of it is taken. But it sometimes happens that a person is not ready to take in the fruit of the sacrament; and such reception of the sacrament is imperfect. Just as the perfect is distinguished from the imperfect, *so too is the sacramental enjoyment—in which only the sacrament is received without its fruit—distinguished from the spirit's joy in which a person also takes in the fruit of this sacrament* and through it becomes united with Christ in faith and in love."

We can see immediately what an enormous difference there is here between the current popular conception and that of the "Common Doctor" of the Church. What Thomas means by sacramental communion is not the physical reception of the sacrament by contrast to the "merely" spiritual reception. Instead, he means the less perfect mode of reception in which only the sacramental aspect of the sacrament is enjoyed and not its real inner core (res sacramenti): quidam suscipiunt tantum sacramentum, quidam vero sacramentum et rem sacramenti. The manducatio sacramentalis means in this distinction the "merely" sacramental reception of the Lord's Supper; it is imperfect in that it does not achieve the perfection that is essential to it. It is precisely the way that the sinner receives the sacrament: "The sinner receives the Body of Christ in a sacramental but not in a spiritual way." And the glossa ordinaria to which Thomas appeals links the distinction between sacramental and spiritual communion to the explanation given by Paul: "Anyone who unworthily eats and drinks is eating and drinking his own condemnation" (1 Cor. 11, 29). Thus the concept "sacramental communion," understood in this distinction, comes close to the concept of "unworthy communion."

On the other hand, for Thomas the concept "communion of the spirit" does not—at least not properly and primarily—mean "merely" spiritual, not bodily sacramental communion, but the genuinely perfect way of receiving the Lord's Supper, in which the bodily sacramental reception is also included.

A Christian can receive the fruit and the real core of the sacrament without bodily receiving the sacrament itself: namely when he has the desire and the intention to receive it in the bodily sacramental way as soon as he can, and so this desire itself can be called a "communion of the spirit" in a derived sense. But we must add and carefully consider that Thomas does not consider this fruitful desire as if it could be aroused at will like some kind of mood. It is, instead, to be seen realistically as desire and its fruit, which only a person can have who is in fact hindered from receiving the Lord's Supper bodily: "Without the intention and the desire to receive this sacrament, salvation is not possible for the person; desire and intention would be meaningless if they were not realized as soon as the opportunity arose": sine voto percipiendi hoc sacramentum non potest homini ess salus; frustra autem esset votum, nisi impleretur quando opportunitas adesset.

How far is all of this removed from any flight from reality into a purely "intellectual" sphere!

Creation and Sacrament
(1951)

In an extremely lively and somewhat challenging book on
Thomas Aquinas, G. K. Chesterton makes the comment
that this great teacher of Christendom should really be
called Thomas a Creatore, St. Thomas of God the Creator.
I think this would indeed be an appropriate characteriza-
tion of the central thrust of St. Thomas's thinking. Loving
acceptance of creation in all its forms and at all its levels
is certainly in line with the principles of his teaching referred to in the famous paragraph 1366 of the Codex of
Canon Law.

This attitude of affirming creation, this acknowledgement of the totality of all real things, is undoubtedly the
core and the central meaning of Thomas's so-called Aristotelianism. This and nothing but this is the root and foundation of that trusting, generous magnanimity which is
the distinguishing element in his ethics. I would even be
so bold as to maintain that this affirmative attitude towards the whole of creation is one of the most important
factors which make him the Doctor Communis Ecclesiae,
the Common Doctor of the Church.

Several kinds of arguments can be cited for having this
attitude to reality—for this "optimism" (so to say). The argument we are most familiar with, the most obvious one,
is the appeal to the Creator Himself who found that the

world He created was "very good." This is not St. Thomas's only argument. However, he uses it expressly and often enough. For example, when he formulates the famous sentence "omne ens est bonum, all being is good" with innumerable variations, the most profound and pronounced of these is that every being, as something real, is wanted and even loved by the Creator; each creature receives this status of being loved along with being real. Again and again Thomas expresses the consequences of this: "Every creature shares in equal measure in goodness as it does in being"; "everything that is, in no matter what way—insofar as it is real, is good"; "evil deeds are good, and from God—insofar as it is a question of their possession of being"; "no matter how much evil can increase it will never be able completely to consume the good"; "the good can be realized in a purer form than evil, for good exists that has no admixture of evil, but nothing is so bad that it has no good in it"; "it is impossible that the good in our nature be completely nullified by sin." The relationship with and the appeal to the Creator are expressed in all clarity in the following text: "Just as natural knowledge is always true, so too is natural love always right. Natural love is nothing but the inclinations of nature planted by the creator of nature: it means, therefore, that it is an insult to the creator of nature if one says that natural inclination is not right."

It is easy to see that the reference back to the Creator is the only legitimate foundation of all "natural law." It is also simply obvious that from the point of view of a supernaturalistic negation of the dignity of all creation the rationale and justification of a natural law is just as impossible as it is, of course, from the point of view of nihilistic atheism, for which something such as creation simply does not exist.

But those arguments based on the doctrine of creation are not the only ones for Thomas, nor even the most characteristic. The most important and the most characteristic argument for justifying Thomas's attitude towards natural created reality—above all, towards the visible world of our senses—is rooted in his theology of the sacraments. Perhaps one may say that the very notion "sacrament" implicitly says that there is a natural, visible created reality which is good in itself, so that, whenever natural created reality is genuinely affirmed, a certain presupposition for a proper understanding of sacrament as such is provided. Conversely, acknowledgement and affirmation of creation can be further supported and strengthened through sacramental theology.

This link between the theology of the sacraments and the affirmation of the visible reality of the world was seen and formulated very early in the history of the Church. Irenaeus, for example, in his book against the heresies lays great emphasis on the fact that it is the first fruits of creation that we offer in the Eucharistic celebration. He says explicitly that at the Last Supper the Lord took bread from the "things produced by this world" and likewise "from this created world of ours" the chalice—by which the Lord wanted to teach His disciples to bring gifts drawn from created things, "not as if God needed them but so that they themselves should not be ungrateful." These words of Irenaeus have no other meaning than that man's gratitude for the natural gifts of visible creation is given its highest expression precisely in the celebration of the sacraments. He says repeatedly that it is the totality of creation that Christ offers to God as a sacrifice.

With these words Irenaeus is opposing the spiritualistic negation of the visible world as it is formulated by the Gnostics. With complete clarity he sees that it is impossible to arrive at a true understanding of the sacraments if one does not at the same time, and first of all, acknowledge the dignity and goodness of the visible world. It is the reality of this world before our eyes which, by virtue of the word of God is so elevated and exalted that it can become the flesh and blood of the Lord.

One misunderstands the "worldliness" of St. Thomas if one is not aware of its theological roots, or, to be more precise, if one is not aware that it is based on the theology of the sacraments. It is his deep reverence for the "fundamental sacrament," for the incarnated Logos Himself that explains his magnanimous "worldliness." Thus Thomas notes in his commentary on John's gospel that it could seem strange to see how John never speaks about the human soul of Christ but only of the Word made flesh. And Thomas asks himself why John would have spoken exclusively about the "flesh." He answers his question with several arguments. The first is as follows: John wanted to prove the reality of the Incarnation against the teaching of the Manichees who maintained that the divine Word could not possibly have taken on a real body because it would have been contrary to God's goodness to take on this "creation of Satan." That was therefore the reason why John expressly and specially spoke of the "flesh": to counter the opinion that the body has an evil origin.

St. Thomas's intention is clear: it is impossible to understand the fundamental reality of Christian faith, the Incarnation of the Logos, without accepting the truth that the visible world and even the "flesh" in which Adam became weak, is fundamentally good.

It is thus not at all surprising that Thomas frequently enough repeats this general thesis in his tracts about the individual sacraments. It would also seem that this insight into the inner connection between the order of creation and the sacramental order stands out all the more strongly as St. Thomas's work nears its end. Precisely the last tract of the *Summa theologica*—which Thomas completed in the last year of his life—is the one in which we find the idea which he had, of course, already formulated in the *Summa contra Gentiles* in very definite and earnest terms: "... so that no one might believe that visible things are bad in themselves and that people who engaged with them were for this reason sinners" (men have sinned—this is not being contested here; and men have chased after visible things—this is not the point at issue here; it is a question of seeing that it is not the inclination to visible things that formally constitutes the sinfulness of that activity; and so Thomas continues): "... therefore it was meaningful that it is precisely in visible things that man is offered the medicine of salvation": in the sacraments.

All of this means: no one can ever grasp the basic truth of all sacramental theology—namely, that the visible things in nature become "real symbols" of salvation i.e., symbols which both *mean* the reality of salvation as well as contain it—unless he presupposes as true that the natural world is good in itself, even "very good," and this on the basis of creation and its origin in the Logos which became man in Jesus Christ. Conversely: the attitude of affirming natural creation finds new and more powerful justification precisely in the theology of the sacraments.

Does all of this have any "practical" application? I think so. There are, above all, two things to speak of here. First: wherever people have no proper sense or not even the slightest notion of the theology of the sacraments and the liturgy of the Church it may be necessary to begin with awakening their understanding of the natural goodness of the natural visible world. Perhaps in this case the main thing is not to promulgate and explain the strictly super-natural truths but to make clear the fact that and the way in which natural visible things—on the basis of their essential natural goodness—are able to become "real symbols" of the highest goodness of God: namely, of his grace.

A second consequence could be: wherever the sense of the liturgy, newly awakened at present, leads to any form of spiritualism, the question should be asked whether the liturgy and the sacraments have really been understood correctly; whether people are aware that—and why—the sacraments presuppose the goodness of visible creation.

Symbol and Trappings
(1938)

1

The seven sacraments of the Church belong to the very core of Christian belief. These words state something which, from time to time, seems to need to be specially highlighted and clarified: that at the core of Christ faith there are seven signs. "The sacrament belongs to the genus of signs"—with these words Thomas Aquinas begins his tract on the sacraments.

If that is the case, a proper and living grasp of the meaning of sign and symbol is a necessary part of the, so to speak, natural presuppositions and conditions for grasping and experiencing the reality of Christian faith. It is necessary to keep the concept "sign" alive in our minds and to preserve its meaning from all confusion and contamination.

The believer's understanding of the sacraments is naturally dependent on its symbolism being correctly understood and meaningfully carried out. In the *Summa theologica* of Thomas Aquinas we read: "Because the sacrament brings about what it symbolizes, the real effect of the sacrament has to be derived from its symbolism." If therefore the sign is not understood, the sacrament as sacrament will not be grasped. And if the sign becomes confused and is not taken seriously, proper access to the understanding of the most central aspects of Christian faith is impaired or even completely thwarted.

Therefore one of the fundamental tenets of the doctrine of the sacraments in classical theology is: oportet in sacramentis significationem servari, "the symbolism of the sacraments must be preserved" (Thomas Aquinas). This principle means that the natural, direct force of the meaning of the sacramental sign has to be realized and to be fully unfolded; that in the performance of the sacraments this natural and direct meaning of the sacramental sign must neither be limited nor overstepped; that the Christian has no other means of correctly grasping the invisible aspect of the sacrament than by "taking literally" the natural and direct meaning of the sacramental sign.

2

We can take a couple of examples from St. Thomas's works to indicate how he himself understood the sentence about preserving the sacramental symbolism and how "literally" he meant it to be taken.

In the *Summa theologica* the question is posed in one of the Articles whether for baptism a real immersion in water is essential. The answer is: no, a mere sprinkling with water is sufficient for the realization of the sacrament of baptism; but using immersion is more "worthy of praise" since through it the similarity with the burial of Jesus is more clearly represented ("All of us who are baptized in Jesus Christ were baptized in His death; through baptism we are buried with Him in his death" (Rom. 6:3)); in the other mode of baptizing this image of the death of Jesus Christ is not so clearly presented.

In the tract about the sacrament of the Lord's Supper we read: from the manifest sign of this sacrament it is clear that taking a meal is the real and primary "function" of the Eucharist; "Bread and wine through which people generally refresh themselves are received in this sacrament as spiritual food." What results from this, for example, is the by no means unimportant observation that the "exposition," the "adoration," and the "visits" are forms of Eucharistic religious practice which are only secondary to the original and essential meaning of the Eucharist.

When, in the short sketch of his teaching about the sacraments in the *Summa Contra Gentiles,* the question is asked in the context of extreme unction whether a criminal condemned to death can receive this sacrament before his execution St. Thomas's answer is no; this anointing can only be given to a person who is really sick. This question might seem to us remote—hardly central. And this is the case. But what is important and enlightening is the justification Thomas gives for his answer: "The sacrament of extreme unction may only be given to a sick person because it is given in the form of physical medicine which is due only to a person who is physically ill. The symbolism of the sacraments must be retained. Just as in baptism washing of the body is required, so too in this sacrament the healing treatment of the physical sickness is required. That is also why the particular material used in this sacrament is oil, for oil has a physically healing effect in that it relieves pain. Thus, too, water, which cleanses the body, is the material used for the sacrament in which a spiritual cleansing takes place."

In his teaching about the sacrament of penance we find a particularly appropriate argument for the seal of confession. As the real and principal reason for the inviolability of the seal Thomas names the necessity of showing the inner core and the fruit of the sacrament of penance as visibly symbolical; all other possible reasons which, to one who is not thinking sacramentally, seem much more obvious, are expressly relegated to a place of secondary importance. It is true that this formulation is from the Supplement to the *Summa theologica*. It is not directly from St. Thomas's own hand, but it is so clearly in line with his own fundamental view that it can justifiably be cited: "In the sacraments that which is externally performed is a sign for that which inwardly happens. And so the confession in which a person submits to a priest is a sign of inner submission to God. But God cloaks the sin of the person who submits to the sacrament of penance. Accordingly, this must be symbolized in the sacrament. Thus it is an essential part of the sacrament that the priest keep the confession secret; and anyone who reveals it sins as one who defiles the sacrament. Other advantages of such secrecy have value along with this basic justification."

In reaction to these examples some might quickly advert to the more pronounced capacity of people in the Middle Ages to work with symbols. But in this context nothing is to be gained from historical commentary. It is purely a question of seeing that the sacraments of the Church of Jesus Christ in which—for all ages—new life is given to people can only be grasped and experienced when they are understood as the Church itself understands them. But when Thomas Aquinas says: "The symbolism of the sacraments must be retained" he is speaking not as a man of the Middle Ages but as the Common Doctor of the Church.

3

Because the sacraments directly perform what they signify and because this effect is, in its existence as such,
bound up with its symbolic presentation, so that, where
there is no visibility of the sign the invisible reality related
to it does not occur—for this reason the inner core of the
sacrament is completely removed from any possibility of
a real "reduction" of meaning. Either the sacrament is really performed and is then complete and intact, or it does
not happen at all. There is no in-between, there are no
steps and grades of more and less. There are, with regard
to man, steps and grades of making visible the invisible
reality; and there are levels of the degree to which the invisible reality is made visible; and there are also levels and
degrees of the live awareness and experience of the sacrament. The thoughts presented here should not be misunderstood or misinterpreted as not realizing that the
sacrament, independently of how profound or weak
human understanding is, is above all something brought
about by God Himself (opus operatum); nor should they
be misinterpreted as saying, absurdly, that the objective
reality of the sacraments of Jesus Christ can be affected or
even threatened by the greater or lesser human capacity
for working with symbols. But it can and must be said that
a Christian is able to sense, to a greater or lesser degree,
the real power—radiated, of itself, with undiminished
force—of what happens visibly/invisibly in the sacrament. It must be said that the flow of sacramental life of
Christians can be either deeper or shallower, stronger or
weaker. And this more or less, this deeper or shallower,
this stronger or shallower is— not exclusively, but primarily—conditioned by the greater or lesser objective

presentation of the sacramental sign in the execution of the sacrament; and in this the objective and the subjective aspects are mutually able to weaken or strengthen one another.

With regard to the objective interpretation and presentation of the sacramental sign, Thomas could today make several observations of this kind: that while the sprinkling with water does not reduce the reality of the sacrament of baptism, the immersion in water expresses more clearly and expressively the mystical reality of what happens in baptism and is therefore "more worthy of praise"; he could, for instance, say that the form of the host used since the Middle Ages in no way compromises the reality of the sacrament of the altar, but that the form of real bread would better and more clearly express the Eucharistic event and would therefore be "more worthy of praise."

However, much more important than such considerations which cannot be directly acted upon is the retention and real development of the symbolism in the performance of the sacraments themselves; it is much more important that in the execution of the sacraments themselves and in the manner of their execution the sacramental sign achieves visibility in as powerful a way as possible. (For it is the point of a sign that it be "seen.") What is important, therefore, is that those who celebrate the sacrament are not merely offered the "abstract" possibility of laboriously understanding and deciphering the sacramental sign but that the visibility of this sign is not easily obscured but becomes brilliantly clear and thereby takes those celebrating the sacrament by the hand, as it were, and leads them to awareness and "love of the invisible reality" and to participation in it. In the Christmas Preface (and also in that of Corpus Christi) we read that the meaning of the Incarnation is that "God, who has become visible, inspires us to the love of invisible reality": precisely this is the meaning of the sacraments which are nothing but the continued, effective presence of the Incarnation of God; as Leo the Great says, "what was visible in Christ" has gone into the sacraments. But for this "inspiration by the love of invisible reality" to be possible the visible aspect—namely, the sacramental sign—must have a visible impact. This process cannot be replaced, even remotely, by a purely verbal "introduction to the liturgy." The most real, most direct, and most generally accessible pointer to the meaning of the sacraments is, instead, the sacramental sign itself. If Mass is not celebrated in such a way that it appears to the believing congregation as a sacred action performed in an irreversible sequence which is directly clear in itself and therefore can be experienced by them; if, for example, the intrinsically necessary meaningful sequence of "preparation for the sacrifice—sacrificial action—sacrificial meal" is confused and the order reversed, perhaps by the sacrificial meal being given at the wrong time, then any instruction about the structure of the Mass, no matter how clever and correct, can hardly expect to be successful. The sentence: "The sacrament contains what it signifies" is equally true in its converse form: the sacrament signifies what it contains. But if the believer "sees" nothing because of the way the sacrament is performed or if he is distracted by seeing something else, it cannot be expected that he will be led by the visible aspect of the sacramental sign to love of the invisible reality. It should furthermore be noticed that in this context we are not merely dealing with a, so to speak, "pedagogical" task of a pastoral kind—for example, to awaken some kind of religious "open-mindedness" or awareness. Instead, it is the primary, central and most binding point of the sacrament itself to be perceived as a sign by the senses and thereby to enable the invisible core of reality to be experienced and grasped.

4

With clarification of the meaning of the sacramental sign (in the strict sense) the most important task has been performed, but there is more. The directly sacramental event is tied into a more comprehensive web of signs. In the celebration of baptism, for example, the directly sacramental action, namely the sprinkling with water in the name of the Trinity, is part of a series of several symbolic acts (breathing on the person in order to chase out the evil spirit and to make room for the Holy Spirit; blessing of the salt which is given to the person to taste; leading of the person into the church under the priest's stole; anointing of the person with holy oil; handing over of the baptismal gown and the baptismal candle). The health or uncontrolled state of this broad area of sacred signs can have a positive and preparatory effect on—or it can work negatively as a hindrance to—the understanding of and sharing in the sacramental event in the strictest sense. In Goethe's autobiography, in Book 7 of his *Poetry and Truth* (Dichtung und Wahrheit), there is a remarkable and beautiful section on the seven sacraments of the Catholic Church. Here we read words we might well take to heart: no Christian can enjoy the sacrament of the altar "with the true joy it is meant to give if the sense of the symbolical or sacramental is not nourished in him." The alertness and health of this symbolic or sacramental sense depends on the sign being realized, properly appreciated and understood in the context of the other actions connected with the sacrament. The proper appreciation and correct understanding of a sign, however, consists in its being "taken at its word"; and the meaningful realization of a sign occurs when it "lets itself be taken at its word," i.e., when its sign value becomes "visible."

If the baptism (for the sake of convenience) takes place not in the church itself but in the sacristy so that the introduction into the sphere of the church, which is meant to symbolize the person's entrance into the community of believers in Christ, is itself only symbolically suggested; and if, furthermore, the words with which the godparent has to answer the questions of the priest as if the person being baptized spoke them were spoken by the sacristan instead; and if, finally, instead of the white baptismal robe by which the innocence of a Christian life in the grace of God is meant to be symbolized a serviette or something similar (which again is meant to symbolize the baptismal robe) is handed to the person—if a baptism is performed like this the symbolism will be devalued and reduced to such an extent that the natural result will be the obscuring of the directly sacramental character. The sacrament will not "be taken at its word" but will sink away into the sphere of the "as if" and "mere ceremony." The reality and validity of the sacrament will not thereby be affected, but by the same token the live understanding and the sharing of the event will be destroyed. This also means acting in contradiction to the sense of the sacraments. The weakening of the "symbolic or sacramental sense" which happens in this way cannot be compensated for by a purely verbal instruction about the meaning of the sacraments.

There is such a thing as a devaluation and debasing of the symbol, making it into a fake. A symbol is a sign that can be taken for what it says. A fake is only the sign of a sign where there is no essential link but only the conventionally accepted sign of a sign. The fake cannot be taken for what it is. The baptismal robe is a symbol; the serviette is a fake.

The only sign which escapes the possibility of such devaluation is the sacramental sign in the strictest and most direct sense. All other signs, even the "sacred signs," are exposed to the danger of degeneration. And even the directly sacramental sign can lose its symbolic force for us—especially when the religious fake has weakened the "symbolic and sacramental sense" in us, when we are no longer capable of being drawn by visible signs to the love of invisible reality. For us, the sacrament will only unfold its full clarity when it is performed and understood, and when surrounded by the complex of sacred signs: as clearly referring to an invisible reality.

5

Today a new capacity for and openness to symbols has been awakened in our people. This is seen also in the religious sphere—and especially in this sphere. It is very important that these new impulses, to the extent that they can be made fruitful in the Christian sphere and in the Church, be applied to the central core of religious symbolism: namely, to the sphere of the seven sacraments. It makes no sense, in the realm of "religious practice," to "reawaken" symbolic actions or to create new ones, unless beforehand, in the sacramental source of all Christian symbols the full force of the sign has again become a living reality for our understanding and experience. Starting from here, one day, in the broader context of Christian life, a genuine symbolic "religious practice" will emerge and established practice will be regenerated. On the other hand, in the Christian religious sphere practices are being encouraged and introduced which do not receive their nourishment from the basic sacramental cell and which are everywhere in danger of building up an illusory fake world—creating a new rampart to hinder the reawakening of genuine sacramental life amongst Christians.

But if the newly awakened openness to symbols leads to (or is led to) the point where Christians learn to take the sacraments "at their word" then something real is gained: things which are primary and necessary. In the face of this it would be feasible to tolerate sobriety and impoverishment with regard to the "religious customs"; it even seems that such a development is characteristic of the times of renewal in Christian history. Whoever is looking to realize something genuine must always, in such times, limit himself to what is necessary and rebuild from there. The core of everything genuine is the essential. What is not essential is a rich development of Christian customs but, above all, that the seven sacraments in which man's salvation is achieved in material signs are understood in all their clarity, and their fruit appreciated and embraced.

Notes 3

For a time during my student days I gave German language lessons to a young Persian. Although he had a fair grasp of ordinary everyday vocabulary it was not always easy for us to understand one another. We had sometimes to resort to the use of a German-Turkish dictionary. This was a bit complicated. One day we were reading together, word for word, an essay in a daily paper dealing with the limitations and sacrifices each one of us had to submit to in the present time. The writer was taking pains to make this comprehensible, if not palatable, to the reader. It turned out that my pupil was completely unfamiliar with the German word for "sacrifice." My attempt at a circumlocution was of no avail, and this, as I know today, was not due to any inability of mine—quite apart from all the problems of language—to say something which communicated the real meaning. I had recourse to our German-Turkish dictionary, looked up the German word and showed it to my pupil with my finger on the line. As I looked at him intently, suddenly his face lit up with a relieved smile. He had finally grasped it. What he then said embarrassed me so much that, without much regret, we gave up our attempt at clarification. My pupil shut the book in relief and exclaimed: "Now I understand. You mean: to slaughter a lamb!" It took me several years to realize that I was the one who needed, in this case, to learn the essential point and that, in this instance, the teacher found himself in the role of the pupil, and a not very docile pupil at that. (1947)

When one reads of human sacrifice among the Aztecs one usually shudders and turns away from such "primitive" abnormalities. But it must not be forgotten that the death of Jesus Christ was a real human sacrifice, and more than the sacrifice of an individual person. And it is necessary for a complete grasp of the essence and meaning of the sacrifice of the Mass that it remain, also in the consciousness of the faithful, related to this human sacrifice. The un-bloody nature of the sacrifice of the Mass is not dependent on its being a sacrifice but on its making present to us the bloody sacrifice (in bread and wine).

The Christian altar is, in its intrinsic form, not only a table but also a sacrificial stone. (1943)

Yesterday in church there was mention of Mass which was to be offered for the whole community and to which, given the difficulty of the age, all members of the community were heartily and earnestly invited. — A strange notion: that one could "offer up" something that had already been offered. It does not really make sense. What is "offered up" in the Mass is Christ Himself (and the community with Him); this offering is the essence of the Mass and without it there is no Mass. This essence is independent of any "opinion" a believer might entertain. It is not affected by whether this offering is shared by him in his subjectivity. On the other hand, of course, it is very important for the faithful that they know about the sacrificial character of the Mass and that their participation in what takes place at the altar is vibrant and alive so that, in a certain sense they too share in the self-sacrifice of Christ, knowing themselves as members of Christ and to this extent offering a sacrifice.

But this is not the "offering" of Mass "for some-thing"—which is often spoken of in Christian preaching as if the Mass were to acquire a special importance for the faithful by virtue of exterior intentions, so that the call for large attendance is based on these reasons.

Such a way of thinking ("offering of Mass," and in-deed "for the community") is, we must fear, only made possible by the sacrificial character of the Mass—the essence of the Mass—not being seen. (1943)

Before their meals the Greeks poured out wine in honor of the gods. — What striking form do we modern people have to express adoration, gratitude, expiation, de-sire for reconciliation? (1942)

With many things we have go back to basics to grasp them in their original meaning.

When my son Thomas celebrated his saint's day yes-terday he was promised by a friend of ours that he would "say an Our Father for him." That is a quite normal and customary way of speaking which, however, says some-thing very complicated and actually meaningless. — It would be understandable if what was said was: I will pray for you and then this prayer was: "God, please hold Your protective hand over this little Thomas Pieper; give him Your grace, happiness in this life, and then eternal life." That would be a nice and meaningful gift for the occasion. But now, what about this praying an Our Father "for" someone? The Our Father is a prayer of adoration, of glo-rification, of surrender to the will of God. It is a petition, but precisely not in the sense of asking something for someone else. Only by undertaking a tricky detour via the interpretation of the Our Father as a "good work" that can be done for another person is it at all psychologically pos-sible to arrive at this construction: "to pray an Our Father for someone." First, (as Pascher has shown in his fine, but badly titled book Inwendiges Leben in der Werkgefahr) prayer is a function of life, the meaning of which is realized as it is lived. Second, precisely the Our Father is so laden with meaning and is by virtue of its origin such a sublime prayer that, given the focus required by the words themselves (directly on the Kingdom of God, on the glorification and sanctification of the Divine name, etc.) a subjective, external "intention" would have to appear extremely unimportant. In its public prayers the Church does not pray the Lord's Prayer for anyone or for any particular intention; least of all does the Church in its liturgy pile up a quantity of prayers and produce a "plus," unless praying the Our Father is seen as an item of work (Pascher). On the contrary, the one Our Father that is prayed in the Mass or in the Divine Office is so prominent and so solemn in word and gesture that repetitions would have to seem out of place. (Let us compare with this the medieval custom of the orders of knights, whose members were required to say the Our Father hundreds of times a day.) A third consideration: such a practice can easily hinder spontaneous prayer as a function of life. Someone who, instead of turning directly to God to express his request, becomes accustomed to such complicated detours, is in danger of losing the ability to make genuine prayers. Naturally, proper and genuine prayers of petition will work in a real hour of need—but then not by a detour via the Our Father, but as a spontaneous cry for help. (1944)

"Liturgical reformers" were often embarrassed when, in a priest who celebrated the mysteries "un-liturgically," they had to acknowledge both a theoretically correct theologian as well as a man of piety in the supernatural sense. — It is not here that the crucial deficit is to be found but in the fact that the "sacramental sense," the organ for the symbolism of creation is lacking: a natural presupposition for the supernatural performance of the sacrament. (1942)

Amongst the elements (or are they only "presuppositions" and conditions?) that constitute the sacramental sense there are at least the following: first, a sense for symbol. Goethe uses the term "symbolical sense" in referring to the sacramental sense.

Second, an awareness of mystery, the conviction that the world has a foundation to which the rational thinking does not necessarily have access.

Third, the sense of rules of the "game," for the kind of action which (in Huizinga's sense) must be called play. This involves understanding why, or rather the fact that there are occurrences, the effect of which is completely bound up with adherence to the most exactly defined rules of behavior (rites), with verba certa et solemnia and prescribed gestures.

Fourth, the sense that there are "powers"—i.e., forces which exist between God and man. (1943)

"All Athenians were initiated into the mysteries, and only Socrates did not undergo initiation because he knew very well that science and art do not proceed from the mysteries and that wisdom is not to be found in mystery. True science is found on the open field of consciousness." This is what Hegel wrote in the *Philosophy of History*. Much and all as it is *Hegel* who is speaking here: the non-sacramental attitude corresponds to Socrates' ethical orientation (as also to that of the "Socratic" Kierkegaard). (1946)

The sacred and the moral order. At Mass on Ascension Thursday last week, by chance the Easter Candle was not extinguished after the gospel. I realized how completely meaningless any excuse would be here ("an oversight," "with the best of good will," "meaning no harm" etc.); excuses have meaning in the moral order in which we are dealing with good will. In the sacred order what is primarily important is the performance itself. Anyone who breaks his fast (no matter how much it is unintended and no matter how much it is accompanied with the greatest longing for the sacrament), cannot go to Communion. And if the Easter Candle, the symbol of the risen Lord being on earth, is not extinguished, something is missing from the Mass on Ascension Thursday. "The good will" of all concerned will not make up for this failure. (Likewise, a breach of the rules in a game is not considered "excusable"; a person who unwittingly and unintentionally breaks the rules of a game pays for it.) A person with a "sacramental sense" will see the difference between the sacred and the moral order. (1947)

Living flame. — This morning, after the Easter High Mass in the chapel, I watched as the altar was "stripped" for the Protestant service which followed. Amongst other things the "eternal" light was switched off again. (...) With a person who is incapable of seeing any essential difference between a wire lit up by an electric current and a living flame it is impossible to speak about elements of the theology of the sacraments. This theology is based on the fact that the symbolic aspect of the visible world is taken at its word and is, first and foremost, even seen! (1947)

In graphology it is an accepted principle that deviation from the norm provided at school constitutes what is characteristic in a person's handwriting. Observing the deviations—their kind and degree—is enlightening also in other ways. — This morning at Mass I heard the woman reading

Mass prayers from the official diocesan prayer book say: "Do not look at our sins but at our good will." In the liturgy of the Mass, which those prayers follow in other respects, it says: "Do not look at our sins but at the faith of Your Church." What a characteristic deviation from the objectively theological in favor of the subjectively moral.

Furthermore, the opposition between "our sins" and "our good will" is not a genuine and meaningful opposition insofar as sin is not an unwitting mistake and a purely objective lapse but precisely a lack of "good will." (1945)

Hollowing out of Eros symbolism in the Christian religious sphere. — When, for example, the Church is referred to as the "Bride of Christ," the word "bride" is understood by today's Christians and theologians as the woman engaged to be married, whereas originally it is clearly the act of marriage—embrace, conception, and procreation—that was meant. This seems to follow from the relationship between Christ and the Church being referred to as the original model for marriage. (1942)

The decline of the sense for the symbolic and the sacramental is seen, if we want to reduce it to the most general formula possible, by the fact that in the early Church there was the danger that a person would "not recognize" the Body of the Lord (1 Cor. 11, 29), i.e., that he would not see the difference between the sacred bread and normal bread. But today the danger is rather that it does not occur to people that under the sacramental signs there is any real bread at all, sacred or otherwise. — The real problem which is at the heart of the sacrament and which must be dealt with by instruction is finding our way from the visible aspect of the sacramental signs to the invisible reality that they signify and contain. But today there is a difficulty—and one which is not essential to the sacramental but is conditioned by a degeneration of the sacramental (insofar as that is at all possible)—a difficulty for people to relate to the visible things (bread, eating, laying on of hands, washing etc.) which would put them on the path leading to the invisible world signified and contained in them. But the rationalist theologian thinks that this invisible world can be grasped and accessed much more directly through abstract reasoning, i.e., without the "detour" via concrete tangible signs. The visible world itself, which according to the Christmas Preface is to inspire us to love the invisible reality, is itself obscured from the searching gaze of the believer. Covered over by the fake, it is made invisible. (1943)

On the concept of participation. — If we want to give reasons for the decline in our sense of the sacramental we will need to distinguish between two different forms of non-participation (in the sacramental event). The first is the lack of attention of the individual who is only thinking of his secular concerns and is taking no notice of what is happening at the altar. The other form of non-participation is, so to speak, of an institutional kind: namely, that the decline of the sacramental sense creates its own "objective" forms and its own social acts which exclude the believer from what is the proper sacramental event. (1943)

The phenomenon that leisure has disappeared includes that fact that people cannot pray. Prayer, as well, gives us escape from the ordinary everyday world and opens access to fundamental realities. The refreshment experienced by the person emerging from prayer is like that of a person waking up from sleep. Leisure-sleep-prayer-contemplation. Seen from this angle, the rule of daily prayer assumes greater importance. (1942)

Once I put together from the Divine Office of the Feast of Michael (8 May and 29 September) what the Church really says about the Archangel Michael. — The first thing is that Michael is called God's designated companion of souls: "Archangel Michael, I have made you the prince ruling over all souls which are to be received." — "Michael the Archangel has come with the multitude of the angels: God has given to him the souls of the saints for him to lead them into the paradise of jubilation." — "The angel Michael, the archangel: God's messenger to the just souls." — "This is Michael, the archangel, the prince of the angelic hosts. Honoring him guarantees gifts of grace to the peoples; his prayer leads to the Kingdom of Heaven."

The second thing is Michael's fight with the dragon (Apoc. 12, 7f.). "When the archangel Michael fought with the dragon the voices of those were raised who cried out: Hail to our God, Alleluia."

There was silence in the heavens when the dragon waged war with the archangel Michael and the voice of the thousand was raised, calling: "Hail, honor and strength to almighty God!"

"Much glory to Michael, the Archangel, who, brave in battle, has won the victory."

Another attribute: "Michael, you guardian (praepositus) of paradise to whom the citizens of the angels' realm give honor."

Helper of God's people: "Michael the Archangel comes to the aid of the people of God; he is there as a helper of just souls."

"At that time Michael will rise up and assist your sons (Dan. 12, 1); a time will come which is like no other known from the beginning down to our own day."

Michael as intercessor: "When John was contemplating the holy mystery, Michael, accompanied by a trumpet, sang: Grant forgiveness, Lord, our God, You who opens the book and its seals, alleluia!"

The angel of the Last Judgment: "The sea was convulsed, the earth shook when Michael the Archangel came down from Heaven."

And finally, in the Lauds hymn: "Angel of peace," "Bringer of serene peace." (1942)

Language symptoms. — A significant newspaper reported, as I could see over the shoulder of a co-passenger on the train, about events on 1 May with the headline: "Day of Confession by all who create in the world." One would have to apply all the tools of interpretation to such typical formulations in order to show what else is implicit in them.

The general level of secularization is seen in the term "Day of Confession." There is no point in talking about the original meaning of "confession" (homologein, repeating words spoken by God—mainly in religious celebration). But even if we begin with the word confiteri—what is really confessed? And in what sense could the utterance in question be called a confiteri?

In the word "create," human and divine activity are put on a par, both understood as "creative"; or rather the sole focus is on human activity which is without hesitation declared to be "creative" (whether it be artistic creation or fashion creations—in both of which there is, of course, an element of invention. And this is a level to which every kind of work, and precisely work that merely executes, is to be elevated). A true example of counterfeit! (1948)

When a call to participation in the services of Holy Week points out that the liturgy of Good Friday is "the oldest and most beautiful of the Church year," it is appealing to the sense of the purely aesthetic, the museum, which is quite opposed to the sacramental sense. The former sense is a dangerously disguised way of not seeing the sacramental signs for what they are—because of the "intellectual" impression it makes. (1943)

"Exactness." — Yesterday, during night watch, I read in an account of the life of St. John Vianney (of Ars-Trochu), that this holy parish priest, whose lack of learning is often highlighted as a pretext, laid great store by exactness in what he said; and he demanded precisely this also of other preachers. — This, and nothing but this, is what we need in the average Sunday sermon—precise statement, not rhetorical ornamentation, not "style" and not panache. Precision. And of course also "genuineness," i.e., directness of personal involvement. Precision and warmth. (1944)

Protestant-Catholic. — J.R. said recently in a conversation that he thought the fundamental Protestant situation was realized in man's extreme exposure as he stands naked before God, for instance in a religious service for prisoners of war in some empty vehicle depot or other. — My answer: for the Catholic religious service, the Mass, at least bread and wine are necessary, i.e., the whole of creation including man. (1947)

Bibliographical Notes

Four groups of my works were not included in this volume.

A first group are the essays of a mainly specialized nature: for example, "Objectivity and Prudence. On the relationship between characterology and Thomistic ethics" (*Der Katholische Gedanke*, 5. Jg.); "L. v. Wiese's fundamental concepts" (*Kölner Vierteljahreshefte für Soziologie*, 9. Jg.); "Sociology as a science of reality. Critical comments on Hans Freyer" (*Archiv für Sozialwissenschaft und Sozialpolitik*, 66. Bd); "The social ideal in the industrial world of work" (Pharus, 25. Jg.).

A second group are essays which were "merged" into later book publications: for example, "Notes on leisure and lack of leisure" (*Die Neue Rundschau*, September 1942); the academic inaugural address "Philosophical training and intellectual work" (published in the periodical *Hochland*, 39. Jg. under the title "Defense of Leisure"); "Meditation on the mirandum" (*Merkur*, January 1950); "The social meaning of leisure in the modern world" (*Review of Politics*, Vol. 12).

A third group are the works which I hope will one day find their place in a larger publication—works such as radio lectures on the themes of "happiness and contemplation" as well as individual essays on figures from Plato's Dialogs (published in *Neue Deutsche Hefte*, 1. Jg.).

Finally, the travel reports, especially the ones about the US and Canada, which are quite voluminous, have been omitted. They were published in the *Rheinischer Merkur* (1950) and in the Hamburg weekly *Die Zeit* (1953).

The Notes are as yet unpublished writings from the World War II years and the time immediately following the war.

I

Knowledge and Freedom. — The text of a speech made at the opening of the International Congress "Wissenschaft und Freiheit" (Hamburg, 23–26 July 1953) which was organized by the "Congress for Cultural Freedom" in collaboration with the University of Hamburg.

The reader may be interested to learn of what for the author was a disturbing experience. A statement by the press almost turned my obvious meaning into the opposite: "… Pieper defended the idea of the pragmatic and therefore unfree character of science" (*Die Neue Zeitung*; 25./26. Juli 1953). "… Pieper, who claimed that the sciences, because of the possibility of their practical application, are not at all free" (*Neue Zürcher Zeitung*; 1. August 1953). *Die Zeit* (Hamburg) spoke of "a sharp attack against the exact sciences": "The exact sciences, he argued, cannot by their very nature be free, for they do not want to be free" (Ausgabe vom 30. Juli 1953). One can see that a high level of publicity—as enjoyed by this Congress with all its technical support—in no way guarantees the reliability of the information.

On the longing for certainty. — Slightly revised text of a lecture given at a celebration on the occasion of the 50th anniversary of the founding of *Hochland* (München, 30. September 1953).

Is there a non-Christian philosophy? Slightly revised text of a radio lecture (Nachtstudio des Bayrischen Rundfunks, München).

Philosophy and Mystery, published in the periodical *Civitas* (Luzern, Oktober 1950).

Philosophy and the Common Weal—published in the periodical Confluence. An International Forum (Harvard University), Cambridge, Mass., vol. I, 1952

Monolog on hope, a radio address at Easter 1951 (Nordwestdeutscher Rundfunk, Köln).

A meditation on prudence, a lecture for radio (Bayrischer Rundfunk, München).

A conversation about simplicity. — The reason why this dialog was not already published throws a somewhat interesting light, I believe, on the inner situation of Christian youth in the "Western" world. What led me to speak about this theme was an initiative of the managers of a large association of young (female) students for whom the question of "simplicity" is of, so to speak, programmatic importance—at least in the opinion of some members of the circle. But then they were opposed so vigorously by another strong group espousing the cause of the ideal of "openness to the present" that my naively invited and, as one might expect, not exactly extremist contribution to the discussion could not be published with the rest.

Chivalry as a soldierly attitude. — These observations appeared in March 1942 in the Berlin magazine *Soldatentum*. At that time the author was employed by the military as an assessor of aptitude. The article was the prompted by the Army High Command—more precisely by the "Inspectorate of the Office for Testing Aptitude," who were familiar with the author's intellectual stance. The employers also envisaged that the article would be a principled view of the shame of the organized crimes against un-armed people on the Eastern front which were beginning to become known in Germany in the winter of 1941/42. Anyone who thinks back to the climate of that time will know that the contrast of bolshevist/Western attitudes with the attitude of "chivalry" could hardly be starker.

The eight "Duties of the German Soldier" dealt with at the beginning of the essay are a kind of introduction to military standing orders (of 1935); they contain, apart from some more external formulations applying to the National Socialist regime, the moral underpinning of sol-diery as embodied, for example, in the figure of Hinden-burg.

What each one of us should do. – A contribution to a dis-cussion arranged by the Nordwestdeutscher Rundfunk, Cologne, New Year's Eve 1951. Other contributors were the Evangelical Regional Bishop Hanns Lilje and Profes-sor Carlo Schmid.

About private property. — This is an essay, translated back from the English, for the public symposium (Fünfer-Symposium), which was organized by the Medieval Insti-tute of the University of Notre Dame (Indiana, USA) for the feast of St. Thomas Aquinas, on 7 March 1950. Each of the speakers had to deal with a text, sent to him in ad-vance, from the *Summa theologica*. The text in each case was provided to the audience in a Latin-English version.

Brief information about Thomas Aquinas—printed in Lexikon des katholischen Lebens (Freiburg i. Br. 1952).

Thomas Aquinas as teacher. — Abbreviated text of a lec-ture held during the "Salzburger Hochschulwochen" in 1949.

"I find I have absolute security." — This title is also the title of a commemorative book of friends (*Gedenkbuch der*

Freunde) which Wilhelm Vernekohl published (Münster 1950) for the tenth anniversary of the death of Peter Wust and in which this article was first published.

Experiment with blindness, written for radio and broadcast on several occasions (Bayrischer Rundfunk, München; Nordwestdeutscher Rundfunk, Köln) was published in the June number 1952 of the periodical *Hochland* (München).

II

Work—free time—leisure was the title of an art exhibition organized by the German Trade Unions (Deutscher Gewerkschaftsbund) and the city of Recklingshausen for the "Ruhrfestspiele 1953." This lecture was held at the opening of the art exhibition.

How does a person learn to see again? — A contribution to an exhibition of school children's work from the Werkschule Münster. It was published in the November volume 1952 of *Baukunst und Werkform* (Frankfurt. M.).

New encounter with a poem. — The author received several written responses to this essay which was published at the beginning of November 1942 in the *Frankfurter Zeitung.* In the essay Wilhelm Klemm, the Leipzig doctor-poet born in 1881, was referred to as the author of the two stanzas; after World War I Wilhelm Klemm became known principally in the circle involved with Die *Aktion,* the periodical published by Franz Pfemfert. By the way, the stanzas treated in the essay are the first two of a longer poem, but even today I would only include these two in my personal anthology.

On music. — A speech made at a Bach Evening of the Pädagogische Akademie Essen (Winter 1951/52).

Published in the May number 1952 of the periodical *Wort und Wahrheit* (Vienna).

III

The greater world. — A lead article in the Christmas edition 1952 of the Hamburg weekly paper *Die Zeit*.

Comments on the missionary situation of the Church in Germany. — My contribution, the open letter of Karl Thieme, and my reply to it were published in the *Werkblatt für die katholische Pfarrgemeinde* (Hildesheim; Jahrgang 1935/36 and 1936/37). Karl Thieme took up the theme again in his book *Am Ziel der Zeiten?* (Salzburg-Leipzig, 1939, S. 197ff.).

On the TV transmission of the Mass. — An advisory opinion, which was a response to the invitation from the Bishops' Commission for Television.

Priesthood and Sacrificial Worship. — This is an answer to a survey conducted by the Pastoral Ministry Institute (Vienna) on the theme "What does the priesthood mean to you? What do you expect of a priest?" It appeared in a special number of the periodical *Der Seelsorger* (Vienna 1953).

Footnotes on the Lord's Supper Tract in the Summa Theologica. — Written down during work on the translation of this tract (published under the title *Thomas von Aquin, Das Herrenmahl* in the Jakob Hegner Verlag, Leipzig, 1937). The *Footnotes* were printed in the periodical edited by Johannes Pinsk *Liturgisches Leben* (Berlin 1937).

Creation and Sacrament. — Translated back from the English of a contribution to the periodical "Orate Fratres"—now "Worship"—(Collegeville, Minnesota, USA).

Symbol and trappings. — The essay had its origins in a "battle" for a worthy performance of the ceremony of baptism of my own children. The rite which up to this point had been the normal one is described in the text without exaggeration. The essay appeared in the December 1938 edition of the periodical *Hochland* (München).

Index

want to value the real human subject, we must never forget that it is also an object and that it therefore exists with an objective structure of subjec-tivity. Hence it is on the basis of the objective structure of subjectivity—implicitly contained in Aquinas—that we can sensibly attempt to recover subjectivity.

This can be described methodologically in several different ways. We could say that it develops the modern theme of subjectivity within the phi-losophy of existence without contradicting it. We could also say that it in-volves not so much reconciliation between the philosophy of being and the modern philosophy of subjective conscience as bringing to mature synthesis the two great currents of Christian thought: the Augustinian-Anselmian and the Thomistic. We might also say that, within Thomistic thought, it involves the development of a more complete anthropology by inserting into the objective consideration of the human person those subjective as-pects of personal relation that Aquinas develops in his teaching on angelic substances and the Trinity, taking care, of course, not to confuse these two levels of personal existence.

Each of these respective definitions contains an element of truth. Taken together, they define a program of philosophical research that in a certain sense goes beyond Aquinas in the direction of modern philosophy, but to-ward modern philosophy on a road indicated by Aquinas as an alternative to the Avicennian-Averroistic road. It is a "modernity" as much aware of "becoming" as it is of "*that which* becomes." Consequently, it is aware of the substantial *unity of philosophy* that runs contrary to the modern mindset, even though it is only by retrieving this substantial philosophical unity that we can address the fundamental questions of reality: i.e., what is the human subject, and what is the relationship between human subjects in a perma-nent, ontic, metaphysical structure?